Get Your Laugh On

JENNIFER KNOX,
PATTY KNOX,
and
MARGIE MCCREADY

WestBow Press books may be ordered through booksellers or by contacting:

WestBow Press
A Division of Thomas Nelson & Zondervan
1663 Liberty Drive
Bloomington, IN 47403
www.westbowpress.com
1 (866) 928-1240

ISBN: 978-1-4908-6895-0 (sc)
ISBN: 978-1-4908-6896-7 (hc)
ISBN: 978-1-4908-6894-3 (e)

Library of Congress Control Number: 2015901633

Printed in the United States of America.

WestBow Press rev. date: 1/27/2016

Series Title Page

Other books by these authors: Keep Your Laugh On
Other material by Jennifer Knox

Complete two year children's ministry curriculum for 1st - 5th grade. Also available in Spanish.

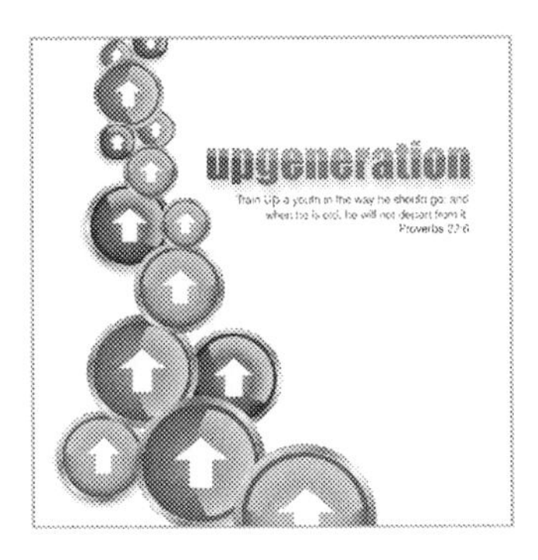

Complete two year children's ministry curriculum for 6th - 12th grade. Also available in Spanish.

Dedication

We dedicate this book to our children, grandchildren, great-grandchildren and all those who follow beyond. You are our joy, our love, our very heart beat. We pray you walk with the Lord all the days of your life. Psalms 102:18 "Let this be written for a future generation, that a people not yet created may praise the Lord."

Acknowledgment

Thank you to Micah Knox, Sarah Annillo, Kim Cushing and Veronica Rush-Eckhardt for all your hours of work in helping us complete this project. We love and appreciate you all.

Also a huge thank you to United NW Church for supporting us in this project. For more information on United NW Church visit unitednw.org.

Preface

I remember the day I picked up the phone and called my mother-in-law, Patty, and said, "We need to write a book!" We had worked together for years in women's ministry at our church, United NW. We had spent over ten years sharing the love of Jesus with ladies through preaching, skits, dances (long story, but these are not your ordinary dances … picture tutus and wigs), stories and whatever else we could think to do.

As the years passed we found that every time we spoke, one of the highlights for the ladies were the times we spent sharing funny stories from our lives. The tears poured down everyones' faces as we would laugh the nights away reliving our misadventures. Year after year we heard the women share how much the night of laughter refreshed their weary souls.

It was from these times of laughter that Patty, Margie, and I have chosen to write this book for each of you. It is our desire that you would be refreshed and encouraged along your life's journey. Each one of us knows the bitterness of life's dark moments, but we also know the gentle touch of our Heavenly Father leading us into His loving arms.

Patty, Margie, and I may not know you personally, but you were on our hearts and minds as we penned the stories on these pages. We pray that you will find refreshment for your soul, laughter in your heart, strength for your body, and most of all that your spirit will soar. May you know the overwhelming, amazing, and powerful love of your Heavenly Father.

In His love,

Jennifer

Biographies

Patty Knox, the wife of Bob for forty-four years and Mother to Jason, Micah, Nathan and Alison, lives in Auburn Washington. She is currently the women's pastor of United NW Church where her son Micah and his wife Jennifer pastor. Patty has been blessed with seventeen grandchildren, plus two more presently on the way. They are to numerous to name but none the less precious! She can also testify to the truth that a "Merry Heart" really does good like a medicine, and that a dose of laughter can be the spoon that administers it.

Margie McCready has been married to her husband, Mark, for 35 years. She is the mother of 5 daughters: identical twins Rachel & Melanie, Corinne, Heather and Hillary. Margie also has 11 amazing grandchildren. She's a homebody and a "nester" who loves to tend to her flowers and wild birds. Her passion is reading.

Jennifer Knox has been married to her childhood sweetheart, Micah, for eighteen years. Together they have four children: Faith, Hope, Grace, and Justice. Jennifer keeps busy homeschooling her children and helping with the children's ministry of their church, United NW. She's had a passion for Jesus since she was very young, and loves having the opportunity to share that passion with others.

Head Held High

Jennifer Knox

Psalms 3:3 But you are a shield around me, O LORD; you bestow glory on me and lift up my head.

It's a moment that's hard to explain unless you've been there, but then, most would never allow themselves to be in this situation! My mother-in-law had yet again convinced me to do some crazy dance for our women's conference. She had already finagled me into riding a bike with her on the back in nun outfits, do a dance in front of a hundred ladies (many who were strangers) wearing a hot pink terry cloth sweat outfit padded with pillows and nylons hanging from our head, and now this! I gave her one of my glares that I so often do just before I head out to fulfill her next crazy idea, but this was almost too much to bear!

My mother-in-law, Patty, had convinced me and another friend of ours that we should do a "Bedtime

Ballet Show" for the women's conference that we were attending. We went through the usual ritual of me refusing her idea, and her somehow hornswoggling me into it. I've never been exactly sure what hornswoggling was, but I'm sure it's what she does to me each time she gets me to go along with one of her crazy ideas! The "Bedtime Ballet Show" would entail us dressing up as elderly women wearing pink tutus, ballet slippers and lots of extra padding in conspicuous places, topped off with wigs and bad makeup jobs. So here I was, ready to go on stage to humiliate myself for the pleasure of others, but that's when the event turned!

The director of the conference informed us that we would need to enter the room through a particular door so that none of the ladies would see us beforehand, making our appearance all the more glorious! The event was taking place at a hotel and we were going to be escorted through the hallway to our destination. I wasn't too surprised as this would be the SECOND time I would find myself in costume roaming through a hotel with my mother-in-law cheerfully leading the way. Only this time was different. Just as we were entering the hallway, we were told that the only way to get to the appropriate door was to go through the entire hotel restaurant! A nice restaurant! A restaurant with people! People who had no idea that there was a women's conference going on in their hotel! No idea why three women would be wearing wigs and tutus! No idea what a great idea my mother-in-law had! No … just hungry people enjoying their nice quiet meals!

It was too late to back out now, I had to make the terrible walk of shame! The only saving grace was that we had brought along fans as props for the dance we were about to do. So I did what any reasonable person wearing a tutu and ballet slippers in a restaurant would do, I covered my face with the fan, kept my head down and walked straight to my destination! I could feel the stares of each person as they saw the bizarre sight in front of them, but I didn't dare make eye contact! The Bible says that the eyes are the window to the soul. It's bad enough that they were seeing me in my tutu, I had no intention of letting them see into my soul!

As we were making our final approach to the doorway, I looked up just long enough to catch a glimpse of my mother-in-law. I knew she must have been feeling pretty bad about her idea and would be ready to offer me an apology, but to my utter amazement … she was walking with head held high, tutu waving in the wind and a bounce in her ballet step! The woman was not only NOT ashamed, she was completely enjoying the moment! People were smiling and she was smiling back … I did notice she made no attempts to make eye contact with me. She knew better!

Within moments, we were ushered into our PROPER room where we were met by a couple hundred highly surprised ladies. We put on a show for them that was actually gut-splitting funny! They laughed so hard that we could hardly hear the music to perform our dance, but dance we did! We remembered all our steps that we had practiced for weeks. The ladies cheered and we laughed till we cried! Patty had yet again brought a crowd to their feet with her ridiculous idea, and at that moment I was so glad I had been a part.

If you are anything like me, you've made mistakes in your life that you wish you could erase. I have often found myself trying to hide from my own shame and failures, but how sweet it is to know that we have a God who says He's the lifter of our head. He can take our ashes and turn them into beauty. He can take our mourning and turn it into laughter! So, the next time you find yourself hanging your head in shame, maybe take a moment to picture my mother-in-law dancing her way through the restaurant, bringing joy to others with head held high! That's the way the Lord wants us to be. Come to Him, let Him wipe us clean, and send us dancing on our way … and yes … with our heads held high!

Close Your Mouth

Jennifer Knox

Ezekiel 16:63 Then, when I make atonement for you for all you have done, you will remember and be ashamed and never again open your mouth because of your humiliation, declares the Sovereign Lord.

The moment is emblazoned on my memory, despite my efforts to forget it. Close your mouth! Close your mouth! The more she said it, the more nervous I became and the more attention from my classmates it drew. Why was my mouth not shutting? It's a picture I'm sure most will not be able to erase. Let me take you back to the fateful moment ... maybe you will have compassion on my humiliation.

When I was in first grade, I got my first set of braces, and yes I just said my first set. I would continue with braces for the next eight years! This particular incident took place midway through my teeth straightening experiment (yup, I was actually an experiment for this particular procedure). I was in fifth grade at Jefferson Elementary, home of the Jefferson Jets! I had recently gotten a new gadget put in my mouth, called a Herbst Appliance (just the fact that it has the word appliance should tell you NOT to put it in your mouth).

"The Appliance" worked like a door hinge on either side of my mouth. One portion hooked to the back top molars, then the other to the front eye teeth on the bottom. I was not informed that the hinge could come apart and if it did, it would need to be put back together (picture a sword in its sheath, if it came out, you would slide it back in … same with "The Appliance"). Since I had no foreknowledge of the dangers of my new "friend," I did what most fifth graders do during a discussion on nouns and verbs, I yawned (hopefully you're not doing that now that I mentioned the "Y" word).

To my utter shock, my mouth got stuck at full yawn! Imagine that the sword came out of the sheath and the edge of the sword got stuck on the edge of the sheath when you tried to push it back into place … it wouldn't go in! That is what my Herbst buddy had done right in front of everyone! There I was with my mouth as wide as I could possibly open it, apparently the doctor had not foreseen a mouth opening that wide and thus not warned me of the hinges coming apart and getting stuck wide … WIDE open!

Now, just so you get a real, clear picture of what trauma I experienced, and am now experiencing as I retell it … try opening your mouth as wide as you can get it. Make sure your cheeks are pulled as tight as possible and now just sit like that while you finish this story. That is what happened to me, only with onlookers! If you are doing my little experiment, you are noticing a very unfortunate side effect, DROOL! When a mouth is pried that far open, it apparently feels the need to drool like a Saint Bernard! Not only that, there is absolutely no way to talk!

So there I was, mouth locked WIDE open, drool pouring down my chin, teacher telling me to close my mouth and me attempting to inform her that "I can't!" To which she would say, "I can't understand a word you're saying, close your mouth!" What is one to do in such a predicament?

Finally, I pointed to "The Appliance" and she came in for a closer look. I saw the horror and I think hidden amusement on her face as she saw the beast in my mouth. She took me to the bathroom and somehow the two of us figured out how to get the hinge back into place. It was a walk of shame back to class with my mouth shut, but sorely cracked lips from being pried open for so long.

As I read this verse in Ezekiel 16:63 "Then, when I make atonement for you for all you have done, you will remember and be ashamed and never again open your mouth because of your humiliation, declares the Sovereign Lord." I was a little curious if the prophet Ezekiel had spoken this about a fifth grader at Jefferson Elementary! However, the Lord is speaking to issues of the heart, not dental issues.

Have you ever done or said things that have left you humiliated and ashamed? Have you ever wanted to take something back, but knew the damage was done? Well, take comfort Dear One … we have a loving Father who "makes atonement" or covers over our wrongs. Atonement actually has its origin from the early 16th century meaning unity or reconciliation between God and man, it was "at one-ment." Regardless of what we have said or done, He wants to cover us and bring us back to His loving arms. And hopefully we learn and next time … close our mouth!

An Obstacle Race

Margie McCready

Psalms 18:29 With your help I can advance against a troop; with my God I can scale a wall.

I was returning home one afternoon from shopping when I noticed a large wooden sign recently placed on the side of the road. It read, "Want to get in shape? Want to lose weight? Want to shed those pounds and look great for summer? Sign up for our Rhody Run training class starting next week at Evergreen Fitness." I immediately perked up. My answers to those questions were, "Yes! Yes! and Yes!." The only problem confronting me was that I was not a runner, I was a walker. I currently am a member of Evergreen Fitness and workout a few times a week. But catch me running down the side of the road? NEVER. I put it out of my mind until the next time I went to exercise and noticed the instructor of the class standing next to the water cooler. As I passed him by I said, "I wish I was a runner, I would sign up for your class." Without changing his facial expression he said, "I can make you one." I just tipped my head back and gave a sarcastic laugh and moved on. About an hour later as I was vigorously pumping my arms on a machine he approached me. "Were you serious about the class?" he asked. "Of course," I said, "who doesn't want to shed pounds and look great for summer? But I don't run, I walk." "Can you walk really fast?" he asked. "Probably faster than anyone here." I chimed in. "Then you would be able to do my class" he said, "you are fit and that is all that really matters."

The sign up sheet was on the front desk. I looked at it for five minutes before I signed on the dotted line. I even paid for it right then so I couldn't back out. I knew me. I would talk myself out of it before I got home. The first night of the class was exciting. Sixteen of us stood around eyeing each other wondering who would be the first to drop out. Sure enough at the second class there were fourteen and by the third class, ten. People were slowly dropping out like flies. During the last two weeks of the class there were only six of us left. My whole body was screaming at me at times and I too wanted to drop out. The only thing stopping me was that I didn't want to be a quitter. At one of the very last classes, we all showed up for another grueling night of fast paced activity that pushed our bodies past their limits. At least that is how we felt. As soon as we got inside, our instructor led us outside to an obstacle course he had set up. My eyes scanned over this monstrous thing and my first thought was, "You have to be joking." I felt like I was in the army and about to enter the war zone. We were put in teams of two. It was great for me but bad for the other person who got stuck with me. I was teamed up with a man named Erik, an engineer by trade and very athletically fit. Unlike me he was a runner. I just looked up at him and said, "I'm sorry Erik." He smiled and said, "You'll do great." I'm sure he was trying to encourage me, but it made me feel worse.

The course was exactly what I imagined it would be; a nightmare! I pushed myself as hard as I could, but to my despair we had to run this for an hour. I remember thinking at one point, "What am I doing scaling walls and running backwards? I'm a Grandma and should be home baking cookies." When we got to the last run I did not think I could keep going because I could no longer feel my legs. I wondered how I was even standing up. Erik could read my face and said, "You can do this." As the horn sounded I propelled myself forward on the legs that I could not feel. To my utter joy Erik was running alongside me, encouraging me and spurring me on. He kept telling me that I could do it and that he believed in me. For me, that made all the difference in the world. He stayed with me until the end.

You and I are in the race of our lives. It is the race of faith. At times we get weary and feel like quitting, but in Christ we can do all things. Because of His mighty power in us we can "run through a troop and leap over a wall" (Psalms 18:29). He is right alongside us cheering us on and giving us what we need to make it. I know it was the Lord who teamed Erik and I together that night. It was his support that allowed me to be able to finish, as I know I would have quit in the final run. It was a great learning lesson for me to remember to reach out and help my Christian friends when they are weary in the race. Sometimes all a person needs is someone else to come alongside them, believe in them and lend a supporting hand.

Swimming In A Rut Puddle

Patty Knox

Psalms 107:35 He turned the desert into pools of water and the parched ground into flowing springs.

"Swim Margie, swim, they like it!," I shouted. Margie, my little sister who was four at the time, thrashed around with fresh new vigor. The year was 1958 and I was just about to celebrate my sixth birthday.

Although we lived on forty acres of waterfront, and with the Big Quilcene river practically at our back door, Margie and I were not allowed to frequent these watering places alone. If we wanted to swim and our older siblings weren't available (or willing) we had to resort to our own water resources, which this particular day happened to be the ruts in our driveway.

We lugged the hose over to a couple ruts that were directly across from each other and filled our troughs to the depth allowed, which was probably just shy of four inches. We had just taken the plunge when our older sister Karen and her boyfriend at the time drove into the driveway in his classic chevy, stopping just a few feet in front of our rut puddle.

What luck, I thought to myself, *An instant audience!* "Swim Margie, keep swimming!" I squealed as I performed some of my own aquatic maneuvers. I quickly glanced up at the car window with its two occupants and discerned my sister Karen's horrified facial expression. *No need to worry big sister, we won't drown*. Guess she wasn't privy to the fact that Margie and myself were skilled swimmers when it came to the art of rut puddling.

"Keep swimming!" I bellowed out. Mainly to calm Karen's concern for our welfare. Margie and I both sprang into action flailing our arms and legs in every direction, spewing mud all over ourselves, not to mention the hood of the car in front of us. Shifting my attention once again to the fans in the vehicle, big sister's facial expression had changed from panic to sheer unbelief (*told ya we were experts in the field of rut puddles*). Not only was she impressed, her boyfriend also, was now stretched over his steering wheel with the same incredulous expression! BINGO!

"Swim Margie, swim, they love it!" Margie in her groove, now flopped onto her back and displayed her famous backstroke emptying half the mud, muck, and mire from her rut puddle.

We kept up our performance until our water had receded to the dangerous level of scratches and empty rut burns. But not until I gave them my grand finale maneuver. A double backward summersault right out of that rut puddle and into my mom's snowball bush. What a superb ending to a marvelous performance!

Waiting now for our grand applause, Margie and myself stood hand in hand before our spectators. Why, we had impressed them so much that it had moved big sister to tears and her man to hysterics! Mission accomplished. Now it was time to receive our rewards (peanut butter and jelly sandwiches). With no obvious sign of an encore coming from the front seat, we headed into the kitchen to claim our prize.

As you have probably already guessed, Karen's tears were not those of pride and admiration but rather shame and humiliation. In fact, big sister's definition of me and little sister's strategically arranged aquatic feats was something like "two little pigs, flipping, flapping and flopping in the mud!" Oh, we didn't hold this against her one bit at the time. Perfectly understandable when one's boyfriend paid more attention to her little sisters rather than wooing her heart.

It didn't take Margie and I very long after to realize rut puddles were not the best places to swim. We soon discovered big buckets and wash tubs held cleaner and deeper water which made for better refreshment. Finally we were allowed access to the river and the bay, which opened up a whole new vista of water gymnastics.

Spiritually speaking, I wonder how many of us have found ourselves swimming in rut puddles. We feel parched and dry, and wanting a quick fix to our thirst and need for water, we drag our hose over to the closest hole we can find. We know it's shallow, and holds murky water. Yet, in our desperate need for refreshment we settle for the the nearest puddle that will quench our thirst. Sometimes if we're not honest with ourselves we will actually believe we are thriving. Before we know it, the rut puddles that once brought us temporary refreshment have now become our permanent water resources.

Jesus doesn't want us to settle for anything less than rivers of living water that He has to offer. In Joshua chapter 15, Caleb gave his daughter Acsah, land. And here was her reply. "Give me another gift. You have given me land in the Negev, now please give me springs of water too. So Caleb gave her the upper and the lower springs. Acsah lived in a dry, arid land but she refused to settle for rut puddles as her main water supply. Cisterns were man made back then to hold rain water that ran off of the rooftop. But the springs of water that Acsah requested came from deep within the ground and delivered clean, pure and cool refreshment.

Maybe it's time for some of us to ask our heavenly Father for those same springs of water, and allow the fountain of His love to refresh our spirits. To submerge ourselves in His word and dive into pools of refreshment that only Jesus can supply. He loves pool parties! Jesus most certainly does indeed! Just ask me and little sister. … "Swim Margie, He loves it!!!"

Becoming Childlike

Margie McCready

Matthew 19:14 Jesus said, "Let the little children come to me, and do not hinder them, for the kingdom of heaven belongs to such as these."

I remember the first time I woke up on May 1st and found a little homemade basket of flowers hanging on my door handle. There was not a note on it and I was puzzled. My husband informed me of the tradition of leaving flowers at people's houses to celebrate the beginning of spring. "How clever," I thought. I absolutely love flowers, a passion inherited from my mother. With nine children to take care of, she took the time to dot our landscape with rows of beautiful bright flowers. I found out two days later the flowers came from Jeffery and David, two adorable little brothers that I took care of at the Christian Daycare down the street. The homemade basket and handpicked flowers became even more special to me. This tradition continued for a number of years until the boys finally reached the age where they no longer considered it "cool." I didn't think I would really miss the flowers every year, but I found myself looking for them every May 1st. It was a reminder to me how special children are. As the years passed, I finally stopped looking.

Fast forward. May 1st, 2010. I came home from shopping to find a beautiful bouquet of light pink Gerbera daisies on my door. I couldn't move for a few seconds, I was delighted. I knew they couldn't be from Jeffery and David as they were all grown up and had moved away. I gingerly picked the flowers up, and sure enough, no note. I immediately put them in water. I discovered a few days later the flowers were from Solomon, my nine-year-old grandson. He learned in school the flower giving tradition and knew how much I loved flowers, so he wanted to bring me some. It was the details of his kind gesture that really affected me. On the morning of May 1st he went to the end of their road and erected a lemonade stand. He then sold his cool drinks for hours, until he had $11.00. Once he had his money, he rode his bike all the way to the supermarket and picked out those flowers himself. He then rode them all the way to my house on his bike and then back home. It took him all day.

Is it any wonder that Jesus said unless we become like little children we won't even get a glimpse of the kingdom? Jesus saw greatness in children. They are humble and have sincere hearts. They are open and teachable, loving and forgiving. They are not self centered and they are free from prejudice and power trips. Children treat everyone equal. They do not get caught up in 'things' like adults do. We can all learn valuable lessons from children. My grandson invested his time and energy as well as his resources to bless me that day. It was an act of kindness and thoughtfulness I will never forget. I saved a petal from one of the flowers and put it in the pages of my Bible. Our faith needs to be childlike. We can all put on the apron of humility and serve others. According to Jesus, that is where true greatness lies.

God's Got A Miracle Waiting On You

Margie McCready

Psalms 77:14 You are the God who performs miracles; you display your power among the peoples.

In the fall of 1978 I was returning home from a Sunday night fellowship time with friends. I had just recently returned to the Lord after wandering in the wilderness for four years and I was excited to be back. Unfortunately I let time get away from me and as I glanced at the clock I discovered it was 11:30 pm. "How are my four year old twins even still awake?" I thought. I scooped them up quickly and headed for home, a town about thirty miles away. Everything was going fine until I rounded a very dark corner about seven miles from home. My car lights slowly started to dim and then went totally out very quickly. My car stopped right in the middle of the road and I couldn't see a thing. There were no street lights anywhere. It was pitch black. My girls were sound asleep in the back seat. I got out of my car and immediately said, "Oh God, help me!" This was a 50 mph zone and I knew I would have to stand in the middle of the road to protect my kids. My heart was racing as about five minutes later I heard a car approaching. I knew if was after midnight and I had remembered my mom telling me once that "nothing good ever happens after midnight." A chill went down my spine. I was waving my arms frantically in the middle of the road when the driver stopped. I could tell it was a man and my heart dropped as I could see he was alone. My fear turned to relief when I heard him say my name as he exited the vehicle! It was a brother in the Lord who had also been at the same home that night and had stayed too long. He drove us home safely after pushing my car off to the side of the road and securing it. When I tucked my girls in their beds I thanked the Lord for His incredible intervention.

The next day after towing my car to the station the mechanic informed me it was the alternator and would cost $136.00 to fix. I was stunned. I was a single mom with very limited funds and he might as well have said a million dollars. I did not have the money.

I needed a miracle. He said the car would be ready in five days. I began to pray and seek the Lord for a miracle. I needed my car.

It was noon on the day I was to pick up my car. I was to be at the station at 1:00. It was about a mile walk so off I went on foot with a few dollars in my purse. I was praying and "looking" at the same time. I was convinced I would find $136.00 at my feet somewhere along the road, or hanging in a tree. "Maybe it will just fall out of the sky." I thought. I really had to exercise my faith as I got closer and closer and could see the station. I was stalling at this point so I decided to pick up my mail since the post office was right across the street. As I opened my mailbox there was one lone envelope in it. It was addressed to me, but my last name was spelled wrong. There was not a return address. The writing was in pencil. I opened it up and shrieked for joy! There was exactly $136.00 in that envelope!! I raced to the station. I even witnessed to the mechanic and showed him my "miracle money." I saved that envelope and put it in my Bible – it has served as a reminder of how wonderful and faithful the Lord has been to me.

Isaiah 46:9 says, "Remember the things I have done in the past; for I alone am God. There is none like me." As we reflect back over our lives, we can see God's faithfulness scattered everywhere. He is Lord over our circumstances and they will take on new meaning and purpose as we trust Him. When we feel ourselves becoming anxious we need to refocus and remember that God is the same yesterday, today, and forever. What He did for us in the past, He can still do today. He does not change. He daily blesses and cares for us. The next time you find yourself in the dark, look up, you just may be on miracle ground.

Jungle Juice And A Rusty Tin Can

Patty Knox

Romans 15:24 I hope to see you while passing through and to have you assist me on my journey there, after I have enjoyed your company for a while.

Camping. Just the thought sent my gag reflexes into overdrive when I was a child. Oh, I enjoyed the "fellowship" of my family at home. It was the journeys that we took together and the provisions for it that always threw me into a dither.

The first source of personal agitation came when everything was packed and loaded in the car for our camping adventures. The last ritual was someone calling out "did anyone remember to get Patty's puke bucket?" Drat! I could already feel the saliva forming on both sides of my jowls while my stomach signaled that motion sickness was about to begin. I say here "about to begin" because I was always sandwiched in the back seat with a pack of siblings that hadn't brushed their teeth before we boarded.

This, and the fact that I got car sick every time our car rolled out the driveway, didn't offer the excitement and adventure that everyone else was feeling. And it surely didn't help the situation to have the rusty old chicken scrap coffee can that doubled for my puke bucket. The moment I got a whiff of that thing I instantly became woozy and before we had left our little town of Quilcene, my head was over that rusty bucket drooling and spitting.

This only confirmed to my dad that it was all in my head until I proved him wrong by barfing in that scrap container numerous times before we reached our destination. Upon our arrival everyone tumbled out of the backseat to explore the new surroundings. Not me though, I was still at the drivel stage; head swirling, stomach rolling, nauseated, not to mention dehydrated. I slowly made my way to the car's edge, hung my legs over, took in a breath of fresh air waiting for my equilibrium to stabilize before I made my next move. This was usually about the time the car was unpacked and the tent was up.

On one particular outing I remember my mom spotted me shortly after our arrival and gave me a cup to get myself a drink. I was starting to feel a sense of relief until I turned on the park's water spigot smelling the yellow sulphur liquid that was trickling out. I felt my nausea wanting to return so I headed over to the picnic table and added to my cup a few squirts of jungle juice to hopefully drown out the smell. Yuck! I don't know what proved worse the water or the jungle juice. Maybe you weren't around when jungle juice was popular. It was flavored syrup that came in gallon jugs with squirt nozzles on the top that you added to water to make a refreshing drink. I hated the stuff, especially the horrible lime flavor. I'm wondering now if maybe its real purpose was for snow cones but mom saw it as a great opportunity to get out of making continual pitchers of Kool-Aid.

Needless to say, I pretty much stayed dehydrated through the entire camping fiasco, and by the time I was clear headed enough to walk a straight line it was also time to break camp and head home. My dad insisted I ride in the front seat with the window open on the return trip but this did not deter my stomach from upchucking. Plus, when we arrived home I had a sunburn over half of my body from hanging my head out the window.

Let me assure you that home never looked so inviting as when we pulled up in the driveway and the engine stopped. I stumbled out and sat on the ground just happy to be back home. The jungle juice disappeared while the rusty old can went back to holding kitchen scraps and I went back to feeling normal.

There is no deep revelation here, just the fact that life itself can feel like one bad camping experience after another. Situations and circumstances can occur that cause us to feel emotionally nauseated and send our heads spinning. Before we realize it, we too have our faces draped over a bucket and it seems like all the jungle juice we add to our cup of suffering brings zero relief. But I have found that like camping trips, trials are seasonal and it just makes coming home more special. I'm especially thankful that Jesus can offer more than a rusty coffee can and some jungle juice. He offers fresh, pure water and a still place to gather our equilibrium!

So Close And Yet So Far

Jennifer Knox

Philippians 3:14 I press on toward the goal to win the prize for which God has called me heavenward in Christ Jesus.

A fifteenth wedding anniversary was a huge milestone for us. In our early years of marriage we had made plans to go to London to celebrate our fifteenth year together. Somehow in our newly budding relationship, we thought it was completely possible to raise a family, buy a house and save enough to go on a European adventure by our milestone anniversary. Needless to say, as the day approached we traded in our European dream for a better reality … Winthrop, Washington!

Winthrop is a small, western-style town about five hours outside of Seattle. From our online research, it looked like the perfect spot for our family to spend our grand getaway. After several hours of driving and a slight detour, we finally made our approach into the greatly anticipated Winthrop!

Always wanting to look my best for my man, I pulled down the visor to get a look in the mirror and refresh my makeup. I could hardly wait to hit all the quaint shops and find the perfect restaurant to dine at. We were all hungry after our long drive, but had decided that we would wait to eat at some cool, western cafe, rather then hit a fast food restaurant on the way.

As I was just putting the finishing touches of my makeup, Micah made a shocking statement! "Well, that was Winthrop!" What was Winthrop? Or better yet, where was Winthrop? We had managed to pass through the entire town while I was putting on lipstick and blush! All we had passed by was a small motel, a gas station, drive through espresso stand and a hardware store. We both agreed that it was false advertisement to have boasted such a bustling, western community, just to find this! No shops, no restaurants, no great adventure!

We took the first turn out of town and headed to the resort we had chosen to stay at. We were all more than a little nervous at what we might find after our sad little western oasis. However, we were all pleasantly surprised at the beauty that awaited us.

The view was spectacular, the hotel beautiful, the food amazing and the pool refreshing (for those who dared to go in, I would not be one of those). For the next two days we lounged around and ate fabulous food, having a wonderful time, but still perplexed over our misguided trip to Winthrop.

On our last morning there, we left our little hide-away and headed back down the mountain to the gas station, espresso shop and hardware store town. We thought maybe there would be a place for breakfast … wrong! We wound up offering our kids gourmet hotdogs from the local convenience store attached to the gas station. How strange that anyone would deem this a destination location! Not even a restaurant!

As we pulled away from our hotdog breakfast location, still laughing about the strange little town, we were met with quite a shock! Before our eyes was the most amazing western town we'd ever seen! It was bustling with people, music and entertainment (well, there was a person playing the harp … a little strange in a western town, but fun nevertheless).

We spent our afternoon exploring all the little shops and taking in the fun that we had hoped for days before. As we were heading home, I started thinking about how so many of us stop short of our destination. Had we traveled just another minute or two down the road, we would have found what we had set out for … but we stopped short.

How about you? Is there an area in your life that you are stopping short of what God has for you? Are you dining on hotdogs at a gas station when a feast is prepared just up ahead? We are on a grand journey in this life and so often we get tempted to settle for less than what God has for us. It may be our marriage, our jobs, ministry, finances, friendship, our children or our relationship with God. Whatever your journey includes, press on to receive the prize that is set ahead of you … and don't stop till you get there!

The Power Of Our Words

Margie McCready

Proverbs 16:24 Gracious words are a honeycomb, sweet to the soul and healing to the bones.

I love honey. I love everything about honey. I love the way it smells, the way it tastes and the way it drips down the back of my throat. I love the fact that it comes from those amazing little creatures the bees. Since God created the bees, then ultimately it comes from Him. I even have a bee man. I get my honey from him in quart jars. He goes by "Captain Mark," as he is a fisherman by trade. Beekeeping is his hobby and eating it is one of mine. The children of Israel ate honey from the rock. It has medicinal purposes as well as tasting sweet! The honey which comes straight from the honeycomb is considered the choicest honey and is called "life honey." It should not surprise us that kind words are compared to honey. When you and I speak kind words to someone, it can soothe their heart and mind which is beneficial to their overall health.

As followers of Jesus Christ, our words should be fitly spoken and minister grace. They should be pleasant to the Lord and to others. Our words should bring life to the listener. We need to think about what is coming out of our mouths. Every day we make choices as to how we are going to use our words. Are we building others up, or tearing them down? Words are very powerful. We can bless with them or curse with them. Our words can become weapons of destruction if spoken carelessly. That is why it is so important that we choose them carefully. Proverbs 12:14 states that, "From the fruit of their lips people are filled with good things, and the work of their hands brings them reward." As we choose to bless others with our words, we will in turn be blessed. Words have a boomerang effect.

My husband works for Alaska Power and Telephone. In Alaska they have a saying: "Three kind words can warm five Alaskan months." If you have ever been in Alaska during their winter season then you would understand the full meaning of this saying. The weather is absolutely brutal. This particular phrase stresses the power that our words carry. A few words spoken in kindness can have eternal value, not only in this life, but in the one to come. Our tongue needs to be an instrument of healing and a communicator of His love.

When My Answers Became My Problem

Patty Knox

Proverbs 16:1 To humans belong the plans of the heart, but from the Lord comes the proper answer of the tongue.

First grade posed a dilemma for me when my teacher, Miss Farrity, informed the class that upon finishing the pages of our lesson we could be excused to recess early. The problem I had with this arrangement was that I dawdled. I got easily sidetracked by flies on the windowsill and kids wiggling in their seats or picking their noses instead of blowing them into a kleenex like Miss Farrity had taught us. I no doubt spent more time poking holes in my paper with the pencil lead than I did writing my abc's. I also spent more time smelling my colors and sniffing my jar of white glue than I did using them. Now, the glue we used was harmless, or so I was told. I never licked the glue stick like Homer or Kenny after I heard the stuff was made from horses. Not sure if that had any validity to it, but I wasn't taking the chance of having my hands and feet turn in to hoofs.

Nope, Miss Farrity's proclamation was not on my list of brainy ideas, but it sure was on Barbara's radar. I knew this about Barbara because she sat in the desk right next to mine. Let me tell you a few more things about Barbara that are worth mentioning. She was totally opposite in her work habits than I was. She loved to do her schoolwork. Not only that, but she was also faster than a speeding bullet and had perfect aim because all her papers had a red A+ splattered across the top! The only thing Barbara failed in was bladder control. She missed that question several times a week and the answer always showed up under her chair. If my memory serves me well, I think that is the only subject that I performed better in than Barbara. I had an A+ bladder!

Well, it was no secret who would be heading out to recess early. Barbara became the queen of the playground in first grade, sinking her royal fanny into whatever swing her heart desired. I had a bird's-eye view of the whole playground kingdom she ruled because I sat near the window too.

Then it dawned on me one day when I was gnawing on my pencil instead of using it, that I too could join Barbara early on the playground. Why hadn't I thought of this idea before? So the next day I sharpened my pencil, sat at attention in my chair and waited for Miss Farrity to distribute the worksheets so I could execute my plan!

When the green light flashed I was off to the races. So was Barbara, she was full speed ahead and hard to keep up with. I think a time or two my pencil was actually smoking. I watched every answer Barbara wrote and copied it exactly. She made letters in the boxes, I followed suit. She drew lines to the pictures and my pencil followed close behind. She crossed T's and I crossed T's. She erased and I erased. I had never worked my pencil so fast and furious in all my six years. Wrist up, wrist up; wrist down, wrist down. I remember at one point pretending we were underwater ballet performers from the way our hands were moving in perfect rhythm.

At last (or should I say quicker than a bullet), Barbara laid down her pencil and took her paper up to the teacher. I knew to hold back and wait until she headed out the door to take my paper up to Miss Farrity, after all, I didn't want to raise any suspicion.

When the coast was clear, I puttered up to the front of the class and proudly delivered my A+ paper.

Miss Farrity looked a tad surprised to see me and then when she glanced down at my work she seemed confused. I knew what she was thinking, that I had it in me all the time to get my papers done quickly and correctly. I waited patiently for this to settle in on her. Then she spoke. "Patty is this your work?" I remember nodding thinking I was so impressing her and at this juncture I was impressed with myself!

Then came the question that I was not prepared for. "Well, since when did you change your name?" Huh? Was this a trick question? I didn't hear her ask brainy Barbara that question. Feeling a little slighted and willing to call her bluff I blurted out "No I haven't changed my name, it is still Patty Newman!" That's when the gavel fell, "Then why, dear, does it say Barbara on the top?" Stink! Double stink! Triple stink with a lick of horse glue, Miss Farrity smelled a rat and it was me!

Needless to say, my carbon copy brainstorm idea didn't get me out to the playground early. However, Miss Farrity in her wisdom remedied my situation by placing me away from the window and Barbara. She sought out a solution to my problem of dawdling too, by letting me erase the blackboard for her if I finished my work by the time class ended. Who knew I just needed something to inspire me? Miss Farrity knew. I had my plans, but my teacher had my answers.

Lord, the next time I have some hair brained idea to come up with solutions to my own problems, help me remember that you have a schoolhouse full of the right ones and I have the green light to copy yours!

Unforeseen Comfort

Margie McCready

Psalms 91:11 For he will command his angels concerning you to guard you in all your ways.

It was a Sunday afternoon in the spring of 2009. My 85 year old dad that I had been helping to take care of since my mom had passed away unexpectedly ended up in the emergency room. We were there for over nine hours as they ran test after test to try and determine the cause of his immense pain. He was admitted to the hospital after they finally located a tumor on his colon. It was decided he needed surgery, and soon. The next few days were very stressful as his weak heart had to be tested to see if it could withstand the surgery. Two days later we were given the green light and the surgery was performed. It was very difficult as the tumor was larger then they expected and it took many hours. My dad did survive the surgery but the recovery was extremely hard on him. For the next two weeks I practically lived at the hospital, arriving very early and leaving very late.

One particular morning I felt more exhausted than usual. My body was lacking proper sleep and nutrition and I was on the verge of tears. I quietly entered his room and sat in my usual chair at the end of his bed. I then said a prayer to the Lord to please help me that morning as my strength was gone. A short time later my dad opened his eyes and then closed them again. He would do this a few times every morning needing the reassurance that I was there. I began to notice that as he was looking at me his eyes were veering a little to the left and then he would smile the most peaceful smile before he closed them again. I had never seen him do this before. He continued to do this during the morning hours until he actually woke up. The first words out of his mouth startled me. "Where is that tall man that was standing next to you?" I replied, "Dad, I have been here by myself all morning." He said, "No you have not, there was a very tall man standing next to you." I knew instantly that my dad had seen an angel. I was overcome with emotion as I shared with him how I had prayed for the Lord to help me, and that the angel he saw was an answer to that prayer.

Angels are our friends in the unseen world. They are messengers sent from God to be with us and take care of us. He instructs them to carry out His purposes. They are commissioned by Him to watch over us and keep us in all our ways.

I then wondered how many times an angel had come to my aid and I was not even aware of it. For some reason that morning the Lord let me catch a glimpse of His amazing love for me. It gave me strength for the challenges I would face in the coming weeks. My dad passed away a few months later, but not before he came to know Jesus Christ as his Savior.

I Feel So Special

Jennifer Knox

1 Corinthians 12:22-24 Those parts of the body that seem to be weaker are indispensable, and the parts that we think are less honorable we treat with special honor. And the parts that are unpresentable are treated with special modesty, while our presentable parts need no special treatment.

OK, time to go back and read the verse above. Do you see how the "less honorable parts" we treat as special? Well, let's keep that in mind as we journey back to my days of swimming lessons!

As every kid does, I could hardly wait for summer to start. I dreamt of warm days playing in our backyard pool, basking in the sun. I was, by my standards, a fabulous swimmer! I could swim laps in seconds without hardly breaking a sweat! Did I mention that our pool was three feet high and about the same across? Apparently, my parents felt that my swimming needed a little boost and signed me up for lessons.

As I arrived on my first day at the public outdoor pool, I stood shivering and wet with about 100 other shivering, wet swimmers. Our first activity was the placement test, no problem for me. We jumped in the pool and began our display of talents. I quickly showed my teacher all that I knew, feeling very confident, I smiled as I completed my test.

I was about to experience my first taste of "The Special Class." It was a class that I would become quite familiar with over the years. I watched as all the students were placed into different levels according to their abilities, I was eager to find out who would be my swim mates for the next six weeks. One by one the kids dispersed to their appropriate areas and began kicking, paddling, and various forms of strokes ... I waited.

One teacher came over to me and introduced himself, "Hi Jenny, I'm Pat and I get to be your teacher!" *Great! Where are all the other students that you get to teach?* I wondered as I looked around with no one in my vicinity. That is when he informed me, "You get to be in a 'special class' all by yourself!" My head swelled with pride that I had made it to the "special class!"

Nobody else had made it there, it must have been all the laps in my pool … practice does make perfect!

As I slid into the pool, holding onto the wall, teacher Pat said we would start by blowing bubbles! I blew and blew and blew! Next we held the wall and kicked our legs … and I kicked and kicked and kicked. Before long, I was kicking and blowing bubbles at the same time! Ahhh, the sweetness of success. When I say "before long," I mean before the six weeks was over. Yup, in six weeks I had tackled and mastered bubbles and kicking! On the last day of class, I watched as all the kids took their tests to pass to the next level. Well, to my delight, if you are in the "special class" you don't need to test … you get doughnuts! I sat on my towel eating my doughnut with teacher Pat, pleased I had mastered … you got it … The Special Class!

The next few summers were much the same, more special classes, more bubbles, more kicking. I just knew that before long I would be letting go of the wall and heading to the deep, open waters. That was the summer of sixth grade when I went to a week of summer camp. It was here that we did the familiar swimming placement test. I knew I could out bubble blow anybody and had confidence that I would do well. I wasn't disappointed I was again accepted into the highly exclusive "special class!" This time we moved on from my usual bubbles and kicking, to the pole!

The pole was a twelve foot pole that stuck up out of the pool and reached all the way to the bottom of the deep end (10 feet down). As all the other kids worked feverishly at learning the crawl stroke, back stroke and butterfly, I worked on holding the pole and seeing if I could go down and touch the bottom!

I think it was about this time that I started to notice that being in the special class may not mean that I was special in the way I had thought. Being almost thirteen and only able to doggy paddle across the pool was a good indicator to me that something in my swim abilities was severely lacking! It was confirmed to me later that summer when I couldn't pass the swim test out of the kiddie pool to go to the big pool. There I was, wading with toddlers in their diapers as my cousins splashed in the big pool, diving off diving boards and sliding down water slides. Don't get me wrong, I showed those diapered swimmers that I could out bubble blow them any day … I still had a little swimming pride in me!

As I eventually grew up and had kids of my own, it was time that I started them in swim lessons and decided to teach them myself to save money. Well, as you can imagine, that didn't go real well since my kids wanted to learn more than kicking and blowing bubbles! They actually wanted to swim! My good friend finally broke the news to me that I had no business trying to teach my kids to swim and needed to get them a real teacher … to which I had to agree!

Well, I may not be able to swim even to this day, but I did learn something from being in the "special class." I am special to the Lord! We are all unique and set apart for His pleasure and purposes! Have you ever looked around and felt alone, like you are doing this Christian walk alone? Just remember, if ever you feel that way … in the "special class" there is only room for two, the student and the teacher. The Lord gives special attention to each of us as His unique creation. We are never alone, we are just getting the best one-on-one training we could ever ask for! And remember … you truly are special to the Lord (even if you can't do the crawl stroke)!

No Need To Fear A Headless Chicken Under Foot

Patty Knox

Romans 16:20 The God of peace will soon crush Satan under your feet.

I was very familiar with chickens while growing up because we had hundreds of the critters that roamed our yard through the years. Every Spring the post office up town would call us on the phone to inform us that our wire packages had arrived and were ready for pick up. This was obvious from the loud chirping sounds that we could easily hear in the background.

Dad would take the old pickup truck to fetch the mail. After what seemed like an eternity to us kids, we spotted dad and his wire packages in the back and followed that truck all the way into the backyard swallowing mouthfuls of dust all along the way!

We raced to see who would spot the first one of those chicken mc nuggets! There they were, a hundred or so of the cutest yellow fluffs with a tiny beak that you had ever seen. Their loud peeping always pulled at my heartstrings and I wanted to give them all a group hug at the same time. I wanted to take care of them and so did my brothers and sisters.

And that is what we did. Morning, noon and night seven days a week. The older the chicks got the older this chore became. As they hit the poultry puberty stage, they lost their cuteness altogether. Have you ever noticed kids at that awkward and gangly stage in their lives? You know, where our teeth fell out and the ones that replaced them looked three sizes to big for our mouths? And our legs suddenly looked like Bambi's, knobby knees and all. While our upper torso could not keep up because our big feet were stealing all the growth hormones? Now morph this visual into a chicken!

Seriously, they go from a cute yellow puffball to gawky, mangy, klutzy, flatfooted creatures. They don't lose teeth because they don't have any, but they do lose baby feathers and it is not a pleasant sight.

And this puberty class of females do not walk normal during this stage of development but rock back and forth and bumble along like a Penguin. Of course, when these hens get to the egg laying stage they suddenly turn sassy. When it was my turn to fetch the eggs, let me tell you these girls did not give up their goods without a fight. Their raucous squawk was followed up by pecks to the hands. They scratched and cackled their way around the yard uprooting all my mother's flowers, and if they took a notion they chased us into the house.

The truth was those chickens were plain ungrateful. We fed and watered them daily, gave them a house with room and board for free, but what did we get in return? Pooped on! That's exactly what we got, whether it came down on our heads from a rafter they were perching on or everywhere else in the yard they could think of so we would step in it. This is why I lost my first love for those critters and this is why I never shed a tear when those birds left the hen house for mom's freezer!

We had a yearly event at our place that drew lots of neighborhood attention. Every kid around showed up for the shindig. It took place in the Fall. We called it "The Newman's Chopping Block Party." This landmark occasion took place out near my mother's clothesline. The weathered chopping block was rolled out of the sticker bushes and placed in a strategic place to allow all visitors an equal view. Then the execution began. My brothers divided up the number of chickens and each took turns wielding the axe. Now lest you think me heartless, I never watched a one, but closed my eyes tightly when I saw the axe handle raised.

Now during one of my shut eye moments I heard and felt a great commotion around my feet only to discover a headless chicken trying to climb my leg. I soon made a beeline around my mother's clothesline and that headless monster chased me not one, but two times around that thing. I tried another route and that thing seemed to follow in hot pursuit! It was not until one of my brothers stepped on it with his foot that it stopped tormenting me.

Isn't this just like Satan's strategy? He roams around like a headless chicken seeking who he may devour. But the truth is, he just tries to scare and intimidate us. Oh yes, he likes to strut his feathers and spiritually chase us around a clothesline a time or two, but the good news is that his flopping about is bigger than his bite.

When Jesus died on the cross for our sins, Satan was placed under Christ's rule and authority. To those of us that belong to Christ this is grand news because not only has Jesus crushed the enemy's head, He also has him under His feet. And that was exactly where that headless chicken needed to be also, right under my brother's feet!

New Creation With A New Do

Jennifer Knox

2 Corinthians 5:17 Therefore, if anyone is in Christ, he is a new creation; the old has gone, the new has come!

I recently received a text from my good friend in Yakima, she was commenting on how much I remind her of another lady she knows. According to my friend Kari, we are both tall, blonde, and wear sparkles … she left out gorgeous with fabulous personalities, but I'm sure that was just a mere oversight.

I chuckled when I read it because it was in response to a text I sent informing her that my son had just asked me what it was like to have a double chin! Not the kind of question I like to engage in. I tried to divert the question by asking, "How would I know?" To which he replied, "Because you have one."

Her text got me thinking about how different people in my life would describe me. If a friend from elementary school was to write she would probably say something like, "She is a tall girl with frizzy brown hair, braces, outgoing personality and loves Jesus." Then, if we were to move to junior high it would sound like this, "She is tall with frizzy brown hair, still has braces, slightly obnoxious personality, outgoing and loves Jesus." By the time I hit high school, "She is tall (good thing I'm not shrinking), frizzy brown hair, insecure but outgoing, and loves Jesus." Seeing a pattern?

However, by the time I reached college things began to change, "She is tall, with somewhat controlled brown curly hair with highlights (things are looking up), a little overweight, confident, very outgoing and loves Jesus." I was able to shake off the insecurity issue once I left high school … I had decided it didn't make a good traveling companion through life.

Then onto married life, "She is tall and pregnant (that was the reality for the first five years), frizzy brown hair (lost the fire to maintain it … too busy with my little ones), not outgoing, somewhat plain and loves Jesus." I look back at pictures and cringe at how I looked. I'll never forget the day that my mom flew in for a visit and informed me that I needed to change out of my pajamas, fix my hair, and put on some makeup. Coming from a very doting mom who always made me feel like a beauty (even frizzy brown haired girls were beautiful in her eyes), I knew I had better clean myself up!

Then it happened! It was that life changing, course altering, world rocking moment … the flat iron entered my life! Goodbye crazy, frizzy hair … hello sleek, beautiful, shiny hair (well, it was never actually sleek, shiny or beautiful but from where I'd come from, it was amazing!)

Now, let me digress here. For all of you naturally, beautiful, shiny hair people, let me give you a piece of advice … don't give advice to those of us with mangled, bristle-pad like hair! One would be shocked to hear how much advice I have received over my lifetime regarding my hair. I have been given more bottles of "Frizzeez" than I care to remember, and for the record, that stuff did NOTHING for my hair. I think those products are for the beautiful hair people who think they know what frizzy hair is when they get a little static going. For people like me, and you know who you are, there is only one cure, actually two: cut it all off, or the better option, the flat iron! Ahh, just the word "flat iron" is giving me chills of delight!

OK, back to the journey through time. If you had asked someone five years ago to describe me they would say, "tall, straight blonde hair (YIPPEE!), friendly, sparkly anything, and loves Jesus." Stick with me, I'm going somewhere with this. Let's move just a couple years back now and ask someone to describe me, "tall, straight blonde hair, sad, withdrawn, insecure, I think she loves Jesus." The hair had finally changed but my heart had too. Life had thrown a deadly blow to me, that at times I thought would completely take me out.

As the Lord so sweetly does, He began the restoring process of healing a very broken heart. It was no magic cure, or miracle prayer, it was (and is) slow, honest and tear filled. I look back now and think, "I'm not even the same person." Ever been there? We do change as life goes on, but our goal should be to change into the image of Jesus.

I don't wear as many sparkles as I used to, I more prefer tennis shoes and sweats these days, my hair (thank you, Jesus) is manageable, I'm still tall, growing in my confidence and security in the Lord, and yes … I still love Jesus! We are all changing and hopefully becoming more like Jesus. We will all have areas that seem like setbacks in our journey with God, but I pray that each of us will allow Him to make us into a better creation than we were before we set out!

Ava Joyce Newman And Her Prize Winning Whistle

Patty Knox

Proverbs 31:31 Honor her for all that her hands have done, and let her works bring her praise at the city gate.

I don't believe there could have lived a sweeter, kinder, or more gentle mother on God's green earth than my own. Even the grand lady who resides on Proverbs Lane at house number 31 could not boast of having more.

My mother never yelled. Having birthed and reared nine children she most certainly had plenty of opportunity. Instead she whistled and corrected by being an example of self control. She never used harsh or unkind words because of our wrong actions, but made a habit of choosing right actions herself to teach us how to make better choices.

She corrected, trained and taught us all valuable lessons throughout the course of her life and she did it through example. My Mother did not have an easy life. The truth is she was well versed in pain and sorrow. Yet I watched as her heartaches transformed her into a wife, mother and friend that was strong in courage and faith. I learned a valuable lesson watching her hurdle over these seemingly impossible circumstances. She taught me that people can be cruel and break your heart but they can never break your spirit and you can always whistle a comforting tune that tomorrow can be better.

I could not begin to tally the number of hours she spent washing clothes and hanging them on the clothesline out back. We always knew when she was there by the happy whistling of her tongue. I remember looking on, puzzled, wondering what could be so pleasant about all the work hanging those items up with clothes pins only to come back and take them down again. Being a mother myself, now I see the lesson she was teaching me. That serving others can be some of the most fulfilling moments in our day.

Mom's cooking was so wonderful that most cooks couldn't hold a spoon up to hers. She produced the best pies, cobblers, cakes, cookies, fried chicken and potato salad in the county. Hot breakfast every morning, yummy lunches and endless hours in the kitchen making special dinners and desserts that followed. Funny thing, I remember her whistling during those times too. Probably because she knew the delight it would bring to our faces when she unveiled her maple bars or homemade bread. The lesson she most wonderfully conveyed to me here is that a selfless heart has its own reward.

I would love to see my mom once more out hanging up clothes and whistling a happy tune, or having her serve me up one last plate of her fried chicken and prize winning potato salad. But she has now passed her baton and whistle on to me to serve my family and hopefully pass on good examples to them. Plus, I know that someday I'll see Mom at her heavenly clothesline and watch her welcome me home with a whistle and a wave.

Many fail to see the great importance and affect that their words and actions have on others. The Bible clearly tells us that life and death are in the power of the tongue. Our words greatly impact and influence people. Oh, that we would all heed this truth and speak only life and encouragement to others.

Our choices also play a powerful role in the lives of children and all those around us. Let us daily ask the

Lord to help us be the kind of examples that will lead people to Him and not away from Him. And finally, let's follow my dear mom's example and try whistling while we work!

God Is In The Apple Pie

Margie McCready

Matthew 6:33 But seek first God's Kingdom, and his righteousness; and all these things will be given to you as well.

When my husband and I were raising our five daughters and living on only one income, money was very scarce in our home. I was a stay at home mom and our girls were in a private Christian school which took out a huge chunk of our income each month. For us it was a priority to have our girls nurtured in a Godly atmosphere. It was well worth the sacrifice.

Eating out for us was a very rare commodity. For my husband and I to go out was even rarer. One evening we received a phone call from a Christian brother who had come into town to spend the day with his elderly mother. My husband and Jim went to high school together and graduated in the same year.

It was suggested that we all go out for a piece of pie at their favorite restaurant down the road.

As we were riding in the car Mark and I discussed how we would split one piece of pie. My husband only had five dollars in his pocket and pay day was still a few days off. The waitress came to our table with a list of fresh pies for us to choose from. As she rattled off the list, one particular pie jumped out at me. It was the apple crumble. When sharing a food dish my husband always let me choose, but on this night I decided not to be selfish and let him choose the pie. I was absolutely convinced he was going to pick the apple. To my dismay he said, "We'll have the marionberry." I was utterly shocked! I wanted that apple pie so bad I could taste it. I began beating myself up for not speaking up when he asked me my preference. I knew right then I had to let it go. Our two guests had been served their pie first. After a few more minutes our waitress came back with our pie, but to my amazement she was carrying two plates. She said, "Ok, we have the apple crumble and the marionberry." My husband then said, "Oh, you've made a mistake, we only ordered the marionberry." Her face puzzled for a moment and then she said, "Oh well, I've already heated it and put a scoop of vanilla ice cream on it so you'll just have to eat it honey," as she set it down in front of me. I was dumbfounded! God and I were the only ones who knew how badly I wanted that apple pie. I knew it was a blessing from Him.

He cares about even the small things and that is what I love about the Lord! He is deeply personal and shows us in very tangible ways how great His love is for us.

Cover Me

Jennifer Knox

Proverbs 17:9 Whoever would foster love covers over an offense, but whoever repeats the matter separates close friends.

For those of you who have had one, you know when you're getting one! Yup, I'm talking about the dreaded bladder infection! It turns a totally normal woman into a pacing wild tiger. Have you ever seen a tiger in a cage pacing back and forth nervously? That is the image I get when I have a bladder infection. Cranberry juice in one hand, phone to the doctor in the other, and all the while pacing, pacing, pacing!

When I woke up at three in the morning with the urge to go to the bathroom, I wasn't instantly aware of what was coming. However, it didn't take me long to know the dreaded situation I was in. No sooner did I lay my head back down on my comfy pillow, when I realized … I've got to go to the bathroom again! Then, the cold reality hit me … NOT ANOTHER ONE! I spent the next four hours waiting for the doctors office to open in total misery.

I was waiting at the front door when they unlocked the office. I was the first patient on the "walk-in" list. To my horror, the walk-ins become "sit-ins." They told me that it could be up to four hours before the doctor could see me. I tried to patiently wait, seeing how they called me "patient Jennifer." However, to their irritation I used the restroom every couple of minutes. I could see the confusion on the face of the male patients who were waiting for the doctor, and the compassion from the female patients.

Finally, my name was called and I was heading to the examining room. There was just one little problem, I had a male nurse! Why did I care if it was a male nurse? The doctor was a male. This should have been no big deal, but for some reason the questions just seemed a little harder for me to answer.

The first question from male nurse, "So why are you here?" My answer, "Ummm a bladder infection." Nurse, "Constant need to go to the bathroom?" "Ummm, no." Nurse, "OK, any foul odor present?" Did he just ask me that? My face turned bright red and I answered a total lie! "Nope, no odor!" Nurse, "Burning while urinating?" Me, "Nope that's fine."

Nurse, "Bowl movements normal?" Me, "Yup, no problem." By the time he finished questioning me I was so humiliated and he was no doubt wondering why I was in there. According to my answers I seemed totally normal! All I could think about was, just give me the urine test and cover my shame!

I did pass that test with flying colors and was given antibiotics. Within a short amount of time I was feeling much better and had returned to normal womanhood. That's when I was able to think about the preceding events with a clear head. Why hadn't I just answered the nurse with the truth? Why was I so humiliated? Best I can figure is that we don't like to be exposed, we want to be covered.

That is what we are to do for each other. Have you ever had a friend that covers you instead of exposes you? One of my closest friends has used our friendship to build me up, lead me to the grace of Jesus and encourage me forward. Other friendships have been used to expose my weaknesses and share my faults.

Jesus is the ultimate friend. He covers all our sins, and leads us in the way of grace. We are meant to be that for others. I pray that each of you will find friends that will cover you and lead you to the Lord. I also pray that in turn, you will be the safe place for others. In the end, may we all find our ultimate safe place in the loving arms of God.

"Hello ... Anybody Home

Patty Knox

Ecclesiastes 4:9-10 Two are better than one, because they have a good return for their labor: If either of them falls down, one can help the other up. But pity anyone who falls and has no one to help them up.

I come by my falling mishaps not by chance, mind you, but strictly by inherited impulses from my dad that landed him a few falls himself. I would describe our actions (mine present but dad's past, since he is no longer with us) as spontaneous. On the other hand, my hubby would agree with the impulse side of both my father and I, but he would rephrase spontaneous impulse to "reckless endangerment!"

Allow me to share with you a situation that happened to my dad a few years back and then you decide if Bob is correct in his assessment of "reckless endangerment"

One thing that stands out to me about my dad was that he was a hard worker all his life. He even worked two jobs at one time to pay medical bills for my older sister, Karen, who had major surgery as a teenager. Dad didn't depend on government handouts. When times got tough, well, he got tougher. He had nine children to provide for, as well as his wife, and provide he did by hunting, fishing, growing huge vegetable gardens, raising chickens and other livestock. To say my dad was busy would be an understatement, Dad was always on one project or another, whether it was chopping wood or building sandboxes. In other words, my dad was very responsible and independent. So even when he got old and feeble, if he wanted something accomplished and the idea suited him just fine, he didn't sit and wait for someone to come along and try to talk him out of it.

The main health problem as he got older was his knees. They had seen better days, as well as his one hip, so he had a hard time getting around and wasn't keen on using a cane. He was also living alone at this time since my mom's passing, but was doing fairly good for the most part. Some of the family tried to set limits on his wandering around the place by himself for fear of him falling, and left their phone numbers by his chair if he needed help. They even purchased him a cell phone of some sort, which I don't believe he ever touched.

Dad loved his dogs. I use the plural here, because he had a pack of them. I kid you not! Six or seven of those beasts surrounded him most of his waking hours. He loved those animals and they loved him! If those mutts were outside for very long and he went to the front porch to do a head count and one wagging tail was missing, he went investigating. (And you weren't going to talk him out of it.)

One day around noon, dad was calling his pooches to lunch. Whole cooked chickens with noodles tossed in were usually on the lunch menu. Breakfast sometimes consisted of pancakes smothered in peanut butter and served individually off metal forks! Believe me here, those dogs were as fat as pigs! Waddled and grunted like them, too. Fat, sassy and living the good life.

So it wasn't a surprise to any of us when dad turned one of his old rentals next door into a doggie lounge, complete with old mattresses and a wood stove that blasted out heat all through the cold winter months. And to make the lounge complete, he had an old radio in the place that tweeted country western tunes! Really! I speak the truth here, just ask my pastor, he has witnessed it too!

That being said, as he called his precious mutts to lunch that day, one of them did not answer with a wag so dad went investigating over at the doggie lounge next door. Now the lounge was in major need of repairs. When you entered the back door, you were in the kitchen, which you had to pass through to get to the lounge itself (keep tracking with me here). The floor was buckling and rotting and very unstable, and as he walked toward the doggie lounge entrance, both dad's feet went through the kitchen floorboards clear up to his hips! Being the independent and resourceful type that he was, he looked for a way out, saw the old kitchen sink and decided to use that for leverage to hoist himself back up (I would have done the exact same thing because spontaneous minds think alike). But the sink was as unsteady as the floor and he jerked it right off the counter, drain pipes and all! Now he was hip deep in trouble with a sink in his lap. I knew what he was thinking at that point, oh yes I did! He was figuring if he was stuck there for some time at least he had a commode available to him (my thought exactly).

Well, after yelping for a couple hours, help did arrive in the form of a grandson who was going fishing in the river close by. Dad was rescued and scolded (went in one ear and right out the other) and the missing mutt was just finishing his lunch when Dad stumbled through the door. Hmmmm, come to think of it, I guess I would have to agree with Bob here. That looks like a case of "reckless endangerment" to me, too. But am I really like my father in this area? You decide.

I had my trusty shovel, my shoes with good tread, gloves, and the plants sitting in front of me that needed separated before going back into the soil. These plants had recently been removed from someone else's garden where they had been in the ground for several years. Talk about root bound and in dire need of separation! As I looked closer at the roots, they appeared to be a hard, massive, tangle of knots. My gut instinct and common sense reminded me then that all the previous falls were preceded by an alert of a fall about to happen. When it went unheeded it was the result of me falling forward, falling backward, falling sideways, go ahead here, you pick the position and I've no doubt rolled that way too! But the idea of waiting until Bob came home to let him tackle the job and the important fact that he had forgotten to hide the shovel from me, also triggered my spontaneous (okay, reckless) side, it alerted me to the fact that Bob was hours away from coming home. Did I really want to wait for 6 hours to get the job done?

I actually wrestled with these thoughts for several moments. In fact, I placed my foot on and off that shovel several times as caution and self control were doing their best to convince me that my foot off the shovel was the best choice. Then without warning, my flesh leaped up onto that shovel with all the force it could muster and went straight through that plant, slicing it right down the middle. I unfortunately went sideways through the flower bed and landed in a heap of dirt!

Why did I do this? I knew better! What would make my lovely, spontaneous nature suddenly switch over to the reckless endangerment side? Very odd behavior, even if it was coming from myself. While thinking through this quandary, but still at a loss for an answer, I decided to dig through my heap pile to make sure I still had all my parts intact and came away that day with a fall that landed me a bazillion bruises and a swollen ankle!

I didn't tell Bob or anyone else in my family what had happened for a few days, because who needs a bruised ego to go along with the ones I had acquired from the fall!

I guess Bob was right about me and my dad after all, but I still don't like to wait on something once I set my mind to do it anymore than dad did. I just need to learn that when my impulses get the better of me, not to act on them unless I'm sure someone else is around. Like the scripture says, "Two are better than one and they can share the work." Plus, it is always nice to have a friend lift you up when you are down and not hide the shovel from you! I'm starting to get it now! Team members working together!.. ... Teamwork! ... ... We are better together!.. ... If one can split a plant, two can split ten!

Now to try and persuade my impulsive side to join ranks with the side of caution. Yikes! I certainly have my work cut out for me, don't I?. ... Guess I'll have to get right on that quick! ... ... Hey! Where's the shovel?

911

Jennifer Knox

2 Thessalonians 2:16-17 May our Lord Jesus Christ himself and God our Father, who loved us and by his grace gave us eternal encouragement and good hope, encourage your hearts and strengthen you in every good deed and word.

It was a day like no other, the day my first child was born. There's really no preparing one's self for what is to come. It is completely unknown territory for a new mom, and that was most definitely true for me. The most I was told is that I would think that I had the most beautiful baby in the world. To me that was ridiculous, since I knew a cute baby from a cuter baby. I really didn't give much thought to what my daughter would look like, I was simply eager to hold her. So what a surprise when she was born and I got my first glimpse of her. I was stunned! I was holding the

MOST beautiful child in the world! I knew parents "thought" they had the most beautiful baby, but I was shocked that I actually HAD the most beautiful baby to ever grace the face of the earth! She was 8 pounds 2 ounces of perfection, topped off with the most adorable dimple. I was completely captivated, to say the very least!

We brought our little girl, Faith, home on December 12th, just one day after she was born. We had already decorated our little house for Christmas, so there I sat on my couch holding Faith, surrounded by sparkling Christmas lights. I had already started a tradition of looking at her, then crying, then kissing her, then crying, then feeding her, then crying ... you get the picture. I did a lot of crying. These were not tears of sadness, these were tears of complete awe, amazement and overwhelming love. Each time I would change her little outfit, I would start the crying process all over again, admiring how cute she was in this new dress, pajama, or onesie.

As I was continuing my crying cycle, I was overwhelmed that I had already had Faith for over a day. How could that have been one complete day? A day pregnant felt like a year! This felt like a second. At this rate, she would be married by dinner! I knew my time with her in my arms would be fleeting, and so I cried again. That's when I noticed that her lips were turning blue. I could feel fear engulfing every inch of my body. I almost felt like my head was spinning as I continued to watch as her beautiful pink lips turned more and more blue before my eyes. I grabbed the phone and called the hospital. I had been there just hours before, but would never have guessed that we would be back there that day.

As the nurse answered the phone, I tried to hold my voice steady as the tears ran down my cheek. I was holding Faith close to me, rocking as I told her about my daughter's lips turning blue. Before she could even get a word out, I asked if I should bring her in myself, or if they wanted to send an ambulance. The words coming out of my own mouth were sending shockwaves of fear through me. "Am I really having this conversation? She's just so little and frail! Oh God, help me, protect my baby!"

It was then that the nurse asked a MOST inappropriate question, "Umm … Mrs. Knox, what is your daughter wearing?" Huh? Did she really just ask me to describe the adorable outfit I have my little angel in? This was serious, and I did not have time for such talk! I pushed past her rudeness and asked again if she wanted an ambulance sent out or if I should drive myself. Completely ignoring my question, she prodded again as to what Faith was wearing. Knowing how urgent the situation was, I answered her as quickly as possible so I could get back to the ambulance question. "She's wearing a little onesie outfit." In irritation, I refused to give her any more details on my daughter's attire. My heart was racing and my body was going numb, but again I forced out the urgent question of what I needed to do. It was then that the nurse gave the final verdict, "Ma'am, your daughter's probably just cold." WHAT!!??? "It's December and she needs to be wrapped in something warm and have a hat on her head. Her lips are turning blue because she's cold."

Although deeply relieved, I was so humiliated! I thanked the nurse for her medical advice and quickly got off the phone. I ran to Faith's room and put her into footie pajamas (no time to cry at how cute she looked this time), wrapped her in three blankets, put a warm cap on her head and sat us both right by the fire! It didn't take long for her lips to turn that soft baby pink again and her rosy cheeks to shine. But then another crisis for this new mom … I think I had overdone the heat and she was sweating profusely! Within minutes her little head was soaked, slicking down the little bit of hair that she had! I knew then, this mom thing was going to be a wild ride. How was I to keep this precious, trusting baby alive, safe and protected … if I couldn't even monitor her temperature?!

By God's grace, and with MANY prayers, my little Faith is now almost 15 years old! I was right when I thought to myself she'd be married by dinner. It seems like yesterday that I was struggling to figure out how to keep her warm. I am ever so thankful that our God has a way of equipping us for every good work. There was no class to prepare me for children. No way of knowing what the love for a child would be like, but in God's amazing grace He has sustained me each day. That's the love The Father has for us. Life will bring many uncertainties, trials and tears, but He has not left us alone. He has sent us the Holy Spirit to counsel and comfort us. If you allow Him, He will walk with you through this life each step of the way … and if ever our hearts grow cold … He knows just how to warm us up in the safety of His arms!

No Chance Meetings

Margie McCready

1 Peter 3:15 Always be prepared to give an answer to everyone who asks you to give the reason for the hope that you have.

It was a beautiful, sunny August morning. I was contemplating what to do for the day when out of nowhere came the thought to go to the little Dollar Store in our town and look for stocking stuffers for my eleven grandchildren. I quickly dismissed the thought as being indoors was not on my radar screen that day. It was too early to be thinking about Christmas! The beach was a much better idea. I was getting things ready for the beach when the Dollar Store thought kept bombarding me. I finally decided just to make a quick stop there. Maybe they got a new shipment of treasures in. It is always a challenge for me to fill so many stockings each year.

I headed down the first aisle when I spotted a very pretty blonde in her thirties. She was extremely thin and looked very fragile. Her face was marked with sadness. I instantly felt compassion for her. I silently prayed as I stopped to browse next to her. I said, "Lord, if I am to somehow reach out to her, then open the door." Sure enough, in a matter of minutes, she asked me a question about an item she was holding in her hand. As we began to converse, she opened up to me. Her husband had just left her and their young son. She had to sell their home and everything in it just to eat. She was staying with friends. Her heart was crushed. He had found another woman to replace her. I wanted to burst into tears as her tears began to flow freely. I knew I couldn't. She needed the Lord. I began to share with her the divine love of God which can heal and transform any life, no matter how broken. I opened up to her and told her I once had also been discarded and tossed aside and I knew exactly the pain she was experiencing. I understood. She reached out and let me pray for her. It was a precious moment. She confided in me that she used to attend a church but she quit going. She left with a seed of hope planted in her heart. She looked different. I knew the Lord had touched her. As she left the store, I stood there in amazement at the leading of the Lord. I now understood why I was to go to the Dollar Store on a hot August day.

I assumed my mission was over so I started to leave that aisle when a man entered the store and made his way towards me. I made eye contact and once again saw incredible sadness. I hesitated. Maybe the Lord wasn't finished after all. He stopped a few feet from me and began looking at the merchandise. I once again silently prayed. In a few minutes he also asked my opinion on an item he was looking at and a conversation started up. He was looking for a gift for his 2 year old son. It was his birthday. He won't get to see him.

His wife left him two months earlier. She took his two sons and went to California. My heart was aching for him. He was truly devastated. His boys were the joy of his life. Then he dropped a bombshell. He said when he got up that morning he had decided to take his own life (as soon as he got the gift in the mail to his son). My heart began pounding. I knew this was a very serious situation and I needed the Lord's heart and mind in dealing with something so delicate. I began to share the love of Jesus with him. At first he was very angry, and non-receptive. I could tell he was angry with God. I understood. I too had been very angry with God once when I was left alone by someone who had promised to love me "until death do us part." It is a very deep wound that only Jesus can heal. I kept sharing how much Jesus loves him when he finally broke down and began to cry. He was a pastor's son! He was also backslidden. I said, "Go home to your father." He said "I can't, I broke his heart when I married a non-Christian woman. He advised me not to. I didn't listen." He was too ashamed to go home. I reminded him of the story of the prodigal son. I said, "Your father loves you and he will welcome you with open arms. There is forgiveness at the cross." It was as if a light bulb went on in his head. I could see a flicker of hope in his eyes. He said, "I'm going home." I was so relieved I didn't know whether to shout or cry. A soul was hanging in the balance that day and God rescued him. He doesn't want anyone to perish. I felt so humbled by the magnitude of what had just happened. What a privilege to get to partner in helping someone down from the ledge.

I stood alone in the aisle. I had never even made it down another aisle and then it hit me. It was never about stocking stuffers at all. It was about hurting humanity who just need to touch the hem of His garment. He was their only hope. It was a divine appointment. How important it is for us to stay alert and move when the Holy Spirit prompts us to. We need to keep tuned in so we won't miss those divine appointments. His ways are not our ways and He moves mysteriously, His wonders to perform. He uses people. We are His hands and feet and voice. We need to be ready to be used at any time in any situation.

I didn't purchase one stocking stuffer that day, but broken lives had been touched by His unconditional love. The Dollar Store became a mission field. Imagine that! It isn't fancy, like Macy's, Nordstrom or some other high end store. Just a humble little dollar store. There really isn't anything of any value inside … nothing over $1.00.

The eternal impact that day?

Priceless.

Looking In The Mirror

Jennifer Knox

> *James 1:22-25 Do not merely listen to the word, and so deceive yourselves. Do what it says. Anyone who listens to the word but does not do what it says is like someone who looks at his face in a mirror and, after looking at himself, goes away and immediately forgets what he looks like. But whoever looks intently into the perfect law that gives freedom, and continues in it--not forgetting what they have heard, but doing it--they will be blessed in what they do.*

It's been almost thirty years since I sat in a patient chair at the orthodontist; it was a seat I was well accustomed to in my elementary school years. I had braces for eight years and went through more treatments than I care to remember. So one would imagine that I must have beautiful straight teeth, but that is not the case! I was told I would need to wear a retainer once I got my braces off, but I was never told that I would need to wear it the rest of my entire life until I reach the grave. So, after a couple months of wearing it, I stopped and well, that is why thirty some years later I found myself back in the orthodontist chair.

I had pondered the idea of getting braces again to fix my teeth, but the entire process seemed too hard and too painful. I can still remember the days of eating applesauce with aching teeth. However, after years of hemming and hawing I decided I was ready for the challenge. My orthodontist had a relatively new treatment that included wearing clear retainers for the course of a year, rather than the traditional braces. I liked the idea of clear retainers that I would change out every ten days, and so it was finally decided that I would go that route.

That brings me back to the chair. I had been laying in the chair for about an hour when the orthodontist told me she wanted me to try putting the retainers in myself. I felt pretty good about the situation and was ready to give it a try. In order to help me see what I was doing, the assistant handed me a mirror. That was when the ever-so-exciting day took a turn! To my absolute horror I noticed that there was something in my nose! Yes … it's what you're thinking! My family calls it a snugar! The dreaded SNUGAR! And right there in front of my orthodontist and her assistant!

What could I do? Here I was laying down trying to put a retainer in my mouth, holding a mirror, but all I could see is what had been in my nose for the past hour! We all know that's what they had been looking at the entire time. I'm surprised they were able to keep their mind on the job at hand with this "thing" in my nose! Since I couldn't do anything about it right then, I had to play it off as if I didn't notice the "thing" in my nose. As I fumbled around my mouth trying out the new dental appliance, my entire body was hot with humiliation! But let me tell you, the very second I was out of sight of that office I was reaching for a tissue to remove the offensive snugar!

On my car ride home the traumatic experience was still fresh in my mind as I relived having to stare in that mirror unable to do anything about what I was seeing. It reminded me of the passage in James 1:22-25 "Do not merely listen to the word, and so deceive yourselves. Do what it says. Anyone who listens to the word but does not do what it says is like someone who looks at his face in a mirror and, after looking at himself, goes away and immediately forgets what he looks like. But whoever looks intently into the perfect law that gives freedom, and continues in it--not forgetting what they have heard, but doing it--they will be blessed in what they do."

I had looked intently into that mirror and let me tell you, I did NOT forget what I had seen! Then I began to wonder how many times I had looked into the Word of God for direction and wisdom, but had not done anything about it. I had not put it into practice. God's Word is meant to be alive in our lives, but that only works when we do what it says. His Word gives us freedom, if we will be faithful to follow it. In fact, if you read it again, it says that we will be blessed in what we do. So, how about we get in the Word today, look intently into it, and then go out and do what it says … there's a blessing waiting for us!

Having A Bird's Eye View

Patty Knox

1 Corinthians 13:12 For now we see only a reflection as in a mirror; then we shall see face to face.

I love to travel to Port Townsend, Washington to visit my sister Margie. She has a quaint home that invites guests to come in and rest a spell. She is also a fabulous cook. Margie has a lovely country flower garden and her front yard hosts a sanctuary for many kinds of birds. When I sit with my cup of coffee gazing out her windows, she is quick to name the different birds that I point out.

Pine siskins, chickadees,toowhees, goldfinches, northern flickers, scrub jays, sparrows, thrushes, grosbeaks, wood peckers, eagles and even two ducks waddle into her yard daily for a visit, and she graciously feeds them all.

She has a tree whose branches envelop the whole front yard and is loaded with bird feeders of all shapes and sizes. In the spring all the birdhouses throughout Margie's yard become baby bird nurseries and the loud echo of chirps can be heard from door to door as mama birds arrive home with breakfast or lunch.

Now, Margie has just one problem with the tree. Its branches reflect off the front windows and from time to time after a bird has eaten its fill from the feeder, it mistakes the reflection for another tree and flies directly into the window.

Some of these poor little creatures lay dazed with little chests heaving up and down but after a while will recover and take flight. Some aren't so lucky. Margie said something about the not so lucky ones that really stuck with me. She said that God attends the funeral of every bird because the Bible declares that He knows every sparrow that falls to the ground.

Just let that settle on you for a minute. If God is that concerned about the little birds He created, how much more does He care for all of us who have been made in His image? Simple but profound truth isn't it?

Now, Margie searched for a remedy to the window reflection problem by purchasing ultra violet reflective strips and attaching them to the upper ledge of her front porch. These strips reflect the natural light turning them into ultra violet rays that are invisible to humans, but not to birds due to the fact that their eyes are twelve times better than ours are. These strips put out a glow that warns as a stop light to birds. Don't you find this fascinating?

This information caused me to realize that we don't always see clearly God's perspective about things and like the birds we can be tricked into seeing counterfeit images and reflections.

Jeremiah 10:14 speaks about the mirrored false images that Satan reflects. We need the help of the Holy Spirit to make us aware of the false mirror that the enemy tries to hold up before our eyes. His mirror is always a counterfeit to the truth of God's holy word. Let me give you an example of Satan's false images.

If you have feelings of low self esteem, low self worth, insecurity, hopelessness, a feeling of abandonment, rejection, feel unloved or alone, then my friend, you have been looking in the wrong mirror. This is a counterfeit reflection of the enemy and false image of who you really are. We must let the truth of the Word and the work of the cross mirror who we really are. Look into the face of Christ, dear one, and see your true reflection!

Standing

Jennifer Knox

Romans 8:31 What, then, shall we say in response to these things? If God is for us, who can be against us?

It's a shock when you go to your mailbox and find an invitation for your twenty year high school reunion! Twenty years! How could that be? It's even more of a shock when you start to realize that you were only eighteen when you graduated, and it's been twenty years since then! It feels like an eternity to get to eighteen. How is it that you blink and twenty years has passed? As I sat staring at the invitation, memories of high school began to flood back. I swore that I would never think about high school or the friends I had there after a terrible senior year.

Up until then, I had always been well liked and made friends easily. I was voted onto homecoming court, elected Student Body Vice-President and then in my senior year was elected President. It seemed as if it was going to be a great year. I was a little sad, because my best friend at the time, Meredith, had already graduated and was now off to college. It was an adjustment not having her there, even more so since we rode to school together every day! Meredith was not only a year older than me, she was funny, super smart and beautiful! It was hard driving myself to school that first day of twelfth grade, no Meredith to laugh with, share deep secrets with, and no Meredith to help me through the year ahead … and what a year it would be.

Memory is a strange thing. After twenty years, I'm not even sure what happened that year. All I know is that my status of having friends and being well liked turned totally around! I've heard that in the animal kingdom, animals prey on fear. That's the best I can figure. It was an almost unbearable year. I was continually ridiculed, talked about and completely shunned by almost everyone. My days consisted of going to school, heading straight to my job, driving back home, and crying. Each day was hard as I was constantly criticized. It was a long, painful year. I would spend my evenings in my room praying and reading my Bible or hanging out with my family. I thank God for my family, they always encouraged, loved and supported me through that long and trying year.

As graduation approached, the school held solo tryouts for the graduation. I'm not sure WHAT I was thinking, but I tried out for a part, and got it! I was set to sing an entire song by myself. As the day grew closer, my nerves were growing more shaky, especially since that was not the only event approaching. My parents separated when I was thirteen and I hadn't seen my dad in over a year. My mom, sister and I lived in Georgia, and my dad lived in Oregon. Relationships were strained and I was extremely anxious about seeing my dad, let alone seeing him and my mom together!

Before I knew it, graduation day was upon us and my dad was in town. I had little time to think about that though, because I was focused on the solo I was about to perform ... perform in front of people who had hurt me so desperately that entire year! When it came time for me to walk up the stairs to the stage, my heart was pounding and my whole body felt numb. Before I knew it, I was staring at a room filled with people, microphone in hand. Then the music started. I scanned the rows of people looking for my mom. I just needed to see my mom! I could feel an entire year of pain washing over me. It was almost more than I could bear. It was then that I saw her. She wasn't sitting where she had been. She had moved into the aisle and was standing up. In what seemed to be a sea of faces, there she was. Standing. The tears came, but by God's grace I was able to sing with all I had within me, because she was standing with me.

I can still picture what she looked like that day, the look on her face, the strength in her eyes. She knew the year I had. She knew the things that had been said and done. She knew I hadn't seen my dad. She knew how hard this moment was, and so she stood. When I felt that I had no one on my side, there she was. She wasn't ashamed of me. She stood for me.

So here I am twenty years later and not much has changed. When it seems that life is too hard for me, and I'm tempted to quit … she stands and supports me. When I've been brought to my knees with heart ache, she stands … and gets me to stand back up. Each time, she points me to the strength that she has held onto, her Heavenly Father. He was the One that held her in her darkest hours. He was the One who imparted strength into her, and He is the One who gives me strength.

If life has brought you a crushing blow and you cannot stand, look up Dear One … He is standing for you. If you let Him, He will pick you up, hold your hand and walk with you. As the Bible says, when you've done all you know to do … stand and know with certainty, He is standing with you.

Exercise Your Way To Laughter And Godliness

Patty Knox

1 Timothy 4:8 For physical training is of some value, but godliness has value for all things.

Our society is crazed with exercise, is it not? There are almost as many exercise gyms as there are coffee stands surrounding us. And when folks are not in the gym doing squats and lifting weights they are outside sprinting, jogging, running and yes, believe it or not some prance like horses! Any adult prancing and trotting around the neighborhood like a young filly is really just making a donkey out of one's self if you ask me. It is one thing for me to see my little grandchildren pretend to saddle up when we go for walks, but if an adult prancer comes hoofing (pun intended) it my way I am moving to the other side of the street!

Then we have the wheel athletics, they ride bicycles, rollerblades and anything else they can attach wheels to. All this hype and public display in exertion has become a popular past time for many seeking that perfect sculpted body.

Now please do not misunderstand me here, I do not have a problem with others getting fit as a fiddle. I have a daughter in law, Eileen who has not only gotten her exercise birthing nine of my grandchildren but also runs marathons!

I must admit up front that I am certainly no spring chicken and if I donned a pair of rollerblades at my age or attempted the horse trot it would certainly generate free entertainment out on the sidewalk. However, this does not mean us old hens don't exercise. We have just chosen an exercise plan that is conducive to our lifestyles while keeping our dignity in check.

After all can you imagine fifty of us old babes on bicycles arrayed in spandex parading down the avenue? How absurd would that be? No, we have more sense and self respect for ourselves than to look like a bunch of partially deflated helium balloons bouncing about on non motorized cycles!

This is why I came up with an exercise plan that helps us senior chicks shed skin and keep our youthfulness. Now, lest you think we are not serious about our exercise plan, I will take you through our daily routine for burning calories and show you what keeps that spring in our steps.

First, let me set the record straight on one thing. You know the old cliche that says "once you are over the hill you start to gain speed?" Well, that is only a half truth, the other half of the equation is because our over the hill bladders are in high gear and you see us racing to the restroom. We also have a familiar gait that is assigned to us over the hill coffee drinkers. When the cafe' au lait or cappuccino decides to kick in we all perform the same well rehearsed turkey strut that beckons us toward the nearest ladies room.

Now, we still do the windmills but without the use of our arms because we are fueled by our gas bloating veggies. Plus, leg lifts are done every time we get in and out of bed. Jumping rope is not a problem, we easily do that when we step over the hose while watering our Geraniums.

Chin lifts are essential at our age. They consist of getting one's ice cream bowl positioned under one's neck and keeping it balanced until the last spoonful of triple chocolate truffle has found its way to our tongue.

We do a couple push ups too every morning before breakfast when we put on our bras. My friend Sandy reminded me that a squat counts every time we get on and off the commode. We execute many of these daily. Yes, even finger exercises are demonstrated every time we work a puzzle, arrange our canasta cards or use the ink blob to blot numbers off our bingo cards!

So you see, exercise doesn't need to be grueling or done in a way that makes a public spectacle of yourself or cause personal humiliation to have its full benefit.

It can be done in the privacy of one's home or with one's friends eating veggies and laughing. Drinking coffee and dancing the Texas two step all the way to the bathroom and back. Do you realize how many calories are burned from just laughing? And not only that, it raises the endorphins to a healthy level giving us the giddy feeling without the Geritol (liquid vitamins for us workout babes over 50).

Belly laughs have also been proven to help in recovery of an illness. The Bible tells us that a cheerful heart is good medicine! Go ahead, read it for yourself. It is in the book of Proverbs chapter 17 and verse 22. This is one of my favorite scriptures and believe me, I have had plenty spoonfuls of laughter in my lifetime that have proven to strengthen my heart.

The Bible reminds us that bodily exercise is of some value and it is good to take care of our bodies for sure, but this scripture also conveys that godliness has value for all things, meaning spiritual fitness is of greater value.

As Christians we should be training to develop not only a godly heart and strong character, but also exercise our muscles of faith by using our God given talents and abilities to help train others to be strong in their faith.

The Lord desires to build endurance into our lives also, so that we can run this race of life all the way to the finish line and receive the "gold medal" that will not fade or perish with time. In all our running have we lost sight of who we are running for? Has a sculpted body become more important to us than a sculpted heart? In our pursuit of strengthening our outer person, are we giving thought to the condition of the person inside?

Let's try to remember that workouts of any kind can profit all of us (yes, even the prancers) if we discern not only the greater value assigned to exercise but also the humor that can be attached to it. Now there is something worth prancing over!

The Do-Gooders

Margie McCready

1 Peter 3:11 They must turn from evil and do good.

When my dad was in his early eighties, his health had reached a point where getting around was very difficult for him. My mother had passed away a few years earlier so I began to reach out to help him. Every Friday I would marathon grocery shop and then drive the 30 miles to his home. My little car would be piled high with huge bags of dog food for his six Labrador dogs. As soon as I would pull up in his driveway, all six dogs in various shades of tan, black and brown would be circling my car. I developed a system that worked well for me. I would grab the bag of pig ears off the front seat to distract them so I could get out of my car and make the many trips into the house. I would hand each one of them this special treat out my car window. I usually didn't see them again for fifteen minutes.

One of the first sentences out of my dad's mouth was, "Well, the do-gooders were here." Who he was referring to were two sisters in their sixties that attended the little church in his small town. Every Sunday after church they would bring him a bowl of soup and bread or crackers. Sometimes he even got dessert if the other church members didn't eat it all first. These two sisters would set him up with a TV tray in front of his recliner (he lived in it) and then one would tackle the kitchen and the other, the living room. Cleaning his house was no easy task. The dogs had the run of the place, so they were continually stepping over and around them, not to mention all their feeding bowls and beds. To make matters worse, his wood stove was always roaring as he liked to keep the temperature in his house at 100 degrees. This helped permeate the air with the smell of dog (it smelled more like 60 dogs instead of 6). It was nauseating. I know. I did it every Friday.

More than the soup, my dad really enjoyed these ladies company. He was lonely. He was also practically deaf, so he would yell to them and they would also yell back. I made sure not to visit on Sundays. The sisters would always share what they learned at church that morning and he listened to them. He respected them because they were living out their Christianity. They were "doers of the word." They were reaching out to the needy. They were being Jesus' hands and feet and it made a difference. They were faithful and he looked forward to their visits every Sunday. I am certain that these women were instrumental in my dad's salvation (he came to know the Lord and passed away a few months later). They even came to see him when he was sick in the hospital with cancer.

Our good works are proof that our faith is real. It is love in action. You and I may never go to a foreign country as a missionary. We may never speak to thousands of people in auditoriums, but we can all be "do-gooders." Jesus went about doing good. So can we. That is our responsibility as followers of Christ. To be a blessing and reach out to help others in any way we can.

Bring the soup.

Wash the dishes.

Pick up the broom.

Visit the sick.

Jesus said it is as if we have done it unto Him. Powerful. The value is eternal.

Putting On The Ritz Doesn't Always Mean The Good Life

Patty Knox

Proverbs: 9:17 Stolen water is sweet; food eaten in secret is delicious!

Boy, oh boy! Did Lady Folly read my mail loud and clear when she described me right alongside herself in Proverbs chapter nine. She calls to all that are like her who lack self discipline. She sits on a seat at the highest point of a city (in my case a tree) and chirps out to eleven year old, stingy, gluttonous girls with boxes of Ritz crackers hidden under their blouses to stop by for a visit. And since I lacked judgment, I answered Lady Folly's call and found myself perched next to her on a branch of the town drunk's maple tree!

It all happened one day when I was up the street visiting with the neighbor girl, Jackie, whom, besides my little sister, was considered my very best friend. Jackie had a small family, just one sister and her mother at home. I, on the other hand, sat around the dinner table every evening staring and sharing with ten other people. Jackie only had to share with her sister Jennifer, so a box of cereal or Ritz crackers afforded her several servings. But not in my cupboard at home. If you got more than one serving of the stuff you really enjoyed, you experienced a double portion blessing that day. Lest you misunderstand me here, my mom was a wonderful cook and we had generous portions of the healthy foods, it's the fun foods I'm talking about. And this particular day, while combing through Jackie's pantry, we spotted a fresh new box of.. … you guessed it, Ritz crackers!

Jackie being five years younger than her sister and having her mom work outside the home, loved to spend time at my house because of all the fun activity. So, she suggested we take the whole box of crackers and head down the street to my place. Now I was agreeable to her first idea about going to my neck of the woods, but I wasn't very keen on the idea of taking those Ritz snacks with us. I could already see eight sets of fingers digging into that box, which meant I would get stuck with only one portion that particular afternoon.

We started toward home and that's when that goofy Lady Folly started yelling something about if I joined her in secret then I could eat to my belly's desire all the tasty Ritz morsels that I wanted.

Jackie must not have been on Lady Folly's radar that day, because she never heard the old bird cawing out her invite. But I sure did and by the time we got to Ginny Hen's (the town drunk's house), which was situated between mine and Jackie's, is when I heard the Folly chick caw even louder about passing by my chance to indulge myself if I kept walking. And before either of us knew it, I had talked Jackie and her box of crackers up in the middle branches of old Ginny Hen's maple tree.

I was desperate for sure, as this was the only suitable hiding place before we hit my front yard, so I had to seize the opportunity. But it was not without risk, however, as we were terrified of Ginny and his staggered wanderings. In fact, if it started getting dark and we had to pass by his place, we ran like two Foster Farm chickens making their break out of the barnyard! I'm sure the neighbor guy was totally harmless, but it didn't help that he lived in a little shack that was covered in sticker bushes. Truth is, Ginny Hen scared the heebie-jeebies out of all the kids in the neighborhood.

But there we were, perched in his tree, with a full box of Ritz crackers which made the dangerous mission worth it all at that particular moment. We cracked that box open and I ate ten to every one of Jackie's. I am ashamed to admit this, but I emptied that box pretty much on my own. I was the stingy glutton that the Bible speaks about that hoards her loot, eats herself silly and then throws it all up! After the last crumb was scooped out of the box, I suddenly felt my gluttonous spirit manifest in my gut! So much so that I hurled from the tree branch I was huddled on, signaling to Ginny Hen if he was home that something bigger than crows were perched out in his tree. If I was lucky, maybe he already had a few swigs under his belt and would mistake us for a couple of stray turkeys. Especially since I had stuffed myself like one!

I remember telling Jackie I must have been bit by a flu bug in Ginny Hen's tree, or some silly thing to that effect, as I stumbled down the old maple tree and now it was my turn to stagger home. Yikes, I was sick! Why, my stomach was turning every which way but the right way. And let's just say here that Lady Folly's ill advice left me in the bathroom throwing up every last bit of Ritz cracker that was a part of my stingy gluttonous experience!

I tell you the truth here, I have not touched a Ritz cracker to this day and it has been over fifty years! I have been coaxed to eat them by well meaning friends. Even my sister, Margie, who is an excellent cook, tried to coax me with a dessert of hers called "hockey pucks" that consist of two Ritz crackers stuck together with a filling and dipped in melted chocolate. But I told myself after that experience that I would no longer place an order with old Lady Folly, especially if Ritz crackers are on the menu! No thanks! Some might ask if I have Ritz crackers in my pantry today and my answer is yes indeed. My hubby and grandkids enjoy them in "moderation". And believe it or not, I have a box of them sitting close by which I just noticed has written in bold letters, "Ritz it up". I don't think so, looks way too similar to "puttin' on the Ritz" and the association could easily bring on a gag reflex.

Just a simple but important truth that I learned from selfishness, a lack of self control and a box of crackers. Stinginess and gluttony are mentioned in the Bible in Proverbs chapter 23 as selfish and excess. These two think only of meeting their own personal desire and cravings. They are self centered, self seeking and self indulgent. Whether it is Ritz crackers, our time, our money, our resources, our talents or anything else that causes us to be self focused instead of God and people focused is Folly indeed!

There is another Dame in the Bible called Lady Wisdom. I've decided her words make a whole lot more sense. She resides on Proverbs Lane, house number 8, and loves company if you should care to visit her. She doesn't have to steal water to taste the sweetness, or eat food in secret to make it delicious. When she speaks, her words are wise and life giving and let's face it, it sure beats trying to put on the Ritz in a tree branch with old pickle-face Folly! Nothing of the good life hanging out with that old bird!

The Secret Note

Jennifer Knox

Amos 3:7 Surely the Sovereign Lord does nothing without revealing his plan to his servants the prophets.

I was throwing up, exhausted, and couldn't be happier! I had just found out that I was pregnant with my husband's and my second child. We already had Faith, who was eight months old at the time, and now a new precious child was on her way. I always loved getting to share the good news with our family. I would call my mom, my sister and dad, since they all live out of state. Then, my husband and I would try and come up with some fun way to tell his mom.

My husband, Micah, and I were quite pleased with our idea of how to share the exciting news of this particular baby. We planned to take Patty, Micah's mom, out to lunch and have a note placed on her food announcing our pregnancy. We spent that morning writing out the note that said, "Congratulations, you're going to be a grandma again!" Then we took it and wrapped it tightly around a toothpick, this was to be stuck into her food. All we needed now was to pick up Patty and head to the restaurant.

I was giddy with delight as we walked into the restaurant and prepared for our little surprise. Patty was unsuspecting as my husband slyly informed our waitress of our plan. The secret note was handed off, we were seated, and my mother-in-law was none the wiser! I was fighting to act normal, as everything in me was running on adrenaline overload at our awaited announcement, when the meal took a surprising turn.

Patty was quite distracted with the cook, which we could all see from our table. After a minute of her continuous glances at the kitchen, she informed us of the cook's inappropriate behavior! "That man is trying to flirt with me!" she informed us with disgust. We were both shocked at her assumption and questioned her on why she thought this was the case. "Ever since we were seated, he's been pointing and staring at me!" It was then that we realized what was going on. We knew our waitress had handed our secret note to the cook to place into Patty's food. With that, I could hold back the laughter no longer! The more she fretted about the flirting cook, the harder we laughed. Patty was aghast at the thought that this man would be so bold! She assumed he wasn't able to see that she was a married woman, a married woman with four children and three grandchildren (and one on the way that she wasn't aware of).

By the time our meal came, she was in a complete dither, but that was nothing compared to her reaction when she saw the little secret note securely wrapped around the toothpick on her plate. "He gave me a note!" she said pointing at the toothpick standing tall in her hamburger. We immediately played naive to the whole thing and said, "That's not a note, that's a toothpick!" "No! No!" she insisted pointing at the paper wrapped around it. "See that! That's a note! He sent me a note! I don't even know if I should read it!" By now, we were wiping tears we were laughing so hard, she assumed it was at the thought of a cook sending her some sort of a love note. She promptly let us know that her heart was for one man, and one man only, her husband Bob. Mr. Flirty Cook was going to have to be told that this grandma was off the market!

So there we were, all three of us, staring at the little secret note shoved into Patty's lunch. Tears pouring down our cheeks, and a flustered mother-in-law, not sure if she should open her secret message. We encouraged her to see if it was a secret message or not, so slowly she unwrapped the paper and held it up for us to see. In a moment of pride that she was correct she informed us, "I told you! See … there's writing on it!" We could hardly respond we were laughing so hard, but we were able to get the words out, "What does it say?" She stared for a moment with a look of confusion as she contorted her face and squinted her eyes to read the little print, "Congratulations, you're going to be a grandma again! How does he know I'm a grandma!" she said with alarm!

We couldn't take it any longer! With gut aching laughter we spurted out our surprise and revealed the true authors of her secret note. Then with head thrown back in delight she laughed along with us. I wonder what the people around us must have thought as we laughed and wiped tears and laughed some more. Our little surprise had turned out to be one of the funniest moments I had ever had. Patty still has that secret note wrapped around the toothpick in her cupboard. What a memory that was!

I've thought about that moment many times throughout my life, remembering the look of horror on my mother-in-law's face thinking the cook was flirting with her then sending a secret message! It reminds me of the fact that we serve a God who says He really does have secret messages to share with us.

Some of His messages we get while studying His word, but others come in those quiet moments when it's just us spending time listening to Him. He says in Amos 3:7, "Surely the Sovereign Lord does nothing without revealing his plan to his servants the prophets." And again in 1 Corinthians 2:10 "These are the things God has revealed to us by his Spirit. The Spirit searches all things, even the deep things of God." I love the way some translations say the "secret things of God." I desire that we would all know the secret things of God. I pray that today you and I will take time to ask what's on His heart, to look deep into His word and maybe, just maybe we will find a secret note.

Oh To See My Mother's Hands Once Again

Patty Knox

Proverbs 31:19-20 In her hand she holds the distaff and grasps the spindle with her fingers. She opens her arms to the poor and extends her hands to the needy.

The scriptures above depict perfectly what my mother's hands represented to me while she was alive. It might sound strange to others to know that one of the things I miss most about my precious mom is seeing her hands. Yes, I truly miss not seeing her face or hearing her voice but to view her hands just one more time has been a secret longing that I have held close to my heart.

I have heard it said that the basic fundamental idea of hands is to communicate in one way or another. We know this to be true in part as hands are able to communicate to the hearing and speech impaired and the blind. Teachers use their hands to compel attention and to instruct in a classroom. Doctors and nurses use their hands to help heal the body, while construction crews signal with their hands to stop or maneuver us on. There is work and responsibility that comes with our hands.

Perhaps this is why I miss Mom's hands so much, because they signaled in a myriad of ways how much she cared for me. Through my memory's eye, I can still see her out at the old clothesline we had in the backyard. It seems like just yesterday that her hands were hanging up the wash, a ritual she did from April when the sun came out until the autumn rains returned. As a small child I would sit on an old stump and watch as she communicated with her hands the work and sacrifice involved when raising a large family.

I witnessed also the endless devotion of those hands preparing meal after meal. And when us kids got measles, mumps and chicken pox she administered healing hands as she nursed us back to health with spoonfuls of chicken noodle soup, sips of cold water, cool washcloths to our foreheads and even cherry cough drops!

Whether it was sharing food, time or popsicles and kool-aid, to all of us and all the neighborhood kids that showed up at our door, Mom's hands communicated love and compassion.

I shudder to think how many diapers her hands changed or how many times they gripped the steering wheel of our old Chevy station wagon to run errands or shuttle us kids from one destination to another. Sometimes she would try to slip away on her own to head to town for groceries just to have a little quiet time of her own. But if I saw that car heading out of the driveway, I would run to the front yard and wait for her to appear while sporting the saddest face a little girl could muster up until mom signaled me with her hand to join her on the front seat.

As I scooted next to her, I loved watching her hands glide the steering wheel all the way to town and back. I felt safe with those hands and I enjoyed her using them to adjust the radio dial to hear Loretta Lynn or Hank Williams senior croon twangy country western tunes across the airwaves!

I trust you understand now why I have yearned to catch sight of them just one more time. Well, the Lord in His great kindness delights in giving us the desires of our hearts and He answered that heart longing though someone else's hands.

It was through a picture that I received recently via e-mail from my sister. She was standing in front of my folk's old apple tree holding an apple with a small object on the top of it. As I zoomed in on the picture I noticed the small object was a little fuzzy black and orange caterpillar atop the apple. I knew my sister was thinking this would bring back fun childhood memories when we collected jars full of these little creatures every fall. But as I looked closer I saw more than fuzzy bugs, I saw my mother's hands!

I couldn't believe what I was seeing. I took in every detail of my sister's hands all the way down to the fingertips. They were a perfect replica of the hands I have longed to see again. Needless to say I smiled and teared up at the same time. What a precious heavenly Father we have that visits the deepest corner of our hearts where our desires are hidden and brings them to life. Now I see my mother's hands every time I visit my sister.

This little story reminds me of some other hands that communicated love and sacrifice by having nails driven into them. Jesus Christ used His hands to demonstrate compassion when He healed the sick and raised the dead to life. And when His hands were nailed to that cross they were extending love and forgiveness of sins to all. Now His hands signal us to come and join Him in his Father's house.

I can hardly wait to see my loved ones in Heaven. I will be watching closely for my mother's hands to click open the pearly gates and welcome me home. God who holds the whole universe in the hollow of his hands also holds us close to his heart.

Mercy And The Willow Tree

Margie McCready

Luke 6:36 Be merciful, just as your Father is merciful.

I looked out the window and saw her and my heart stopped. She was coming down the road towards our house and I knew I was in trouble. I had done it again! She had asked me a million times to stay out of her tree as I was breaking the branches, but I couldn't resist. It was a hot summer day and I was sitting under the shade of this magnificent weeping willow tree. It was my favorite of all trees. I loved how it looked and how the branches swayed in the wind. My friend Jackie lived right next door to Opal and the two yards were connected. The tree was on the border of the two yards and we loved to sit under the shade of this tree and talk for hours.

It was a Sunday afternoon and we were laughing and conversing without a care in the world until I remembered I had a geography assignment due the next day. I had to color a map of the United States and it had to be in colored pencil. I didn't have those particular pencils and asked Jackie if she had some I could borrow. "I do," she said, "but they are at school." I was doomed! I couldn't afford another bad grade in this class. I absolutely despised geography and my report card proved it. I decided to head for home when the tree got the best of me. I looked at Opal's house. It looked deserted. I didn't even see their car in the driveway. So I did it. I climbed and I hung and I swung on those branches with all my might. I felt free in that tree. Now I was going to pay for that short burst of freedom.

As she began getting closer to the house, I did what any 10 year old would do in my position. I ran as fast as I could and hid in my room. I heard the knock and my Mom opened the door. "Is Margie here?" she asked. I almost swallowed my tongue. "I'll get her," I heard my Mom say, but I was sure I was well hidden. I was wrong. The walk to the front door felt like a death march. My heart was pounding and I felt like I was going to faint. I couldn't look her in the face. I knew I was guilty. My eyes rested on a box of colored pencils she held in her hands! I was stunned! I looked up at her and she said, "I heard you needed these and I won't be using them."

Opal was in her 60's. The pencils were brand new. I felt like a heel. She not only heard me, but she saw me swinging in her precious tree again. I deserved to be punished, but instead, I received mercy. She returned good for evil. That was my first encounter with a true Christian who loved the Lord with all her heart.

All I knew is that she went to church and was "religious" (whatever that meant). She demonstrated the love of Christ to me that day by her act of kindness. I couldn't speak and my eyes filled with water. She understood and handed me the pencils. I watched her walk slowly back down the road until she was out of sight. I was shocked by her kindness to me. Giving me what I didn't deserve. Exactly what Jesus does for us. Gives us mercy instead of judgment. It is called grace, and not one of us deserves it.

I got an A on my geography paper. I handled those pencils very carefully as if they were valuable, because they were. At least to me. I kept them in a special place. I never climbed in her tree again. Her house is empty now, but the tree still remains. I wish Opal was alive so I could thank her. Not only for saving me from getting an F on my paper, but demonstrating to me what Christianity is all about. Forgiveness. I'd like to show her that the Jesus she showed to me that day, I came to personally know and love. I have tried to follow her example by returning good for evil. Who knows? It could just make a difference in someone else's life; an eternal difference. It did to this 10 year old's.

The Old Grey Mare She Ain't What She Used To Be

Patty Knox

Proverbs 16:31 Gray hair is a crown of splendor; it is attained in the way of righteousness.

I recently celebrated my 60th birthday and should be indulging in the celebratory fact that I get all the discounts now due to my "senior citizen club status." Especially since I love to shop for bargains. I must admit that it is nice to get the senior perks while I am out and about. Even getting my meal discounted when I go out for lunch or dinner is a grand gesture from the restaurant community. However, between you and me, it is a wee bit humiliating when the waitress brings you a special menu alongside your grandchildren's and now you both have something to color on. This and the fact that they offer your discount at four o'clock daily. What's that all about?

Is turning 60 the official "happy hour" at the all you can eat salad bar? And why do they have to call it the early bird special? Do they hope we will read the sign and eat like one? This could ruffle my tail feathers if I had any … I suppose they assume we go to bed at dusk like the birds, too (not happening with this old night owl).

To tell the truth, this stereotyping of us seasoned chicks is a little hard on the old gizzard, but getting older and being robbed of one's body parts only to see them resurface in strange places is not sitting pretty with this old hen and I'm crying fowl! So, what's all the squawk about, you ask? Well, read for yourself one elderly woman's theft report and you'll soon see what I mean.

I went to bed as usual one night and woke up the next morning only to throw back the covers and realize a theft had been committed. Someone had stolen my legs right from under me and left me with two split rails. Not only that, but they had the audacity to scoop cottage cheese taken from my very own refrigerator and smear it all over the upper part of those split rails! I quickly began taking inventory of the rest of my anatomy and to my horror realized the thief had let the air out of my upper arms also and they looked like two deflated balloons hanging off my shoulders.

If that wasn't disconcerting enough, in my distress while getting dressed, I accidentally put my pants on backwards and they fit! (You know the cute little story of the runaway pancake. Well, I have news for you. That's not just a story and there is nothing cute about it because that rolling flapjack happens to be my stolen hind end!)

Now, I will also inform you that this is not just an isolated case with me, either. The thieves are still on the prowl and targeting my fellow senior sisters. Why, just the other morning I was at a checkout line (yes, exercising my senior citizen club status) and I noticed a senior babe next to me turn her head just enough to cause me to see she had been robbed too. That poor lady had her eyebrows snatched right off her forehead and in their place were two pitiful pencil attempts to cover up the stolen property! And that same day while pulling out of the store parking lot, sure enough, I spotted a little granny pushing a cart whose neck had been pilfered and replaced with a turkey's! If that's not alarming enough, just today while sitting in the doctor's office, I sat next to a lovely, older woman with beautiful white, but thinning hair holding a magazine pulled close to her face. When her name was called, she bent over to place the magazine back on the coffee table and that's when I realized she was victim number four! How was I privy to this? Because the missing hair from the top of her head was now sprouting out of her chin! Who would do such a trick as to rob a dame of her tresses and move it to her face in the form of a goatee (sick and wrong in my book)! This villain must be brought to justice and the sooner the better.

The talk circulating at the "happy hour salad bar," is that perhaps the thief is in cahoots with the restaurant industry to try and prevent us senior babes from utilizing our senior citizen discount status. The bingo gang have their own theory and think the retail industry is part of the conspiracy. All I know is we want our body parts returned to us and these shenanigans behind us!

Ok, so I am fudging with you about the theft report, but I have come to realize that as we age our bodies seem to morph into a creation of their own. We seem to lose parts we want to keep and gain parts we want to lose. Isn't it so all you seasoned sisters? You know full well what I am talking about. You younger babes, your turn is coming.

I asked the Lord one day to show me the positive perks of growing old, if there were any, and to my surprise and delight He opened up His word and caused me to see that old age is not a curse, but a blessing. The first place He led me to was in Proverbs 17:6 where it states "Children's children are a crown to the aged." BINGO! We would not be able to experience the delight of grandchildren if we didn't grow old, nor wear a crown given to us because of them. The Lord gently reminded me also that my crown held seventeen irreplaceable jewels so far. Hmm Lord, maybe my focus was on what I thought I was missing rather than what I had gained in return.

The Holy Spirit also pointed me to Job 12:12 where it talks about wisdom that is found among the aged and that long life brings understanding. Plus, in chapter 15 of Job, it speaks about gray hair and old age being on our side. How so? The Bible teaches that a long life is a sign of God's blessing and all that comes with it. Do you know that there is a treasure chest full of scriptures that speak about wisdom and honor belonging to the aged?

So, I have decided to change my perspective toward getting older. I proclaim from the Bible that gray hair and old age are blessings, because with it comes experience and wisdom to be treasured and graciously passed down to the young. I see also now that gray hair is not a sign of weakness to be covered over, but a crown of splendor to reflect God's faithfulness. And what proud granny doesn't want to sport a crown that displays all her grandchildren? Can I get a hearty amen from all you fellow grandmothers out there? Good! Now wear that crown under that gray head proudly. Celebrate in your senior citizen status and I'll meet you at the "four o'clock early bird special all you can peck at salad bar!" Who cares if we have missing or misplaced parts? We have been given in their place wisdom, life's grand experiences, and treasured grandchildren that can only come with old age and gray hair!

Yes, indeed, I am beginning to understand the perks that come with living a long life, aren't you? I can see that getting older is something to be embraced and not to shrink back from. And I think I have gained a better understanding of the meaning of gray hair and the splendor that comes with it. Aptly put, THE OLD GRAY MARE AIN'T WHAT SHE USED TO BE … SHE'S BETTER! … … However, if it's all the same to you, Lord, I'll still continue to have my daughter, Alison, toss in a little color from time to time as I'm sure you are wild about older brunettes, too!

Did You Just Yank Out My Tooth

Patty Knox

Ecclesiastes 3:2 A time to plant and a time to uproot.

If you are like most people you would just as soon summit Mount Everest in place of going to the dentist. But not me, not this brave, hang tough, don't feel a thing patient (or so I thought until just recently).

Now before this time, I was extremely comfortable sitting in the dentist chair. This was most likely due to the fact that I frequented the office every four months or so and have kept up this tradition for many years. In fact, I have become so familiar with the whole routine that I'm sure I could give myself the shot of numbing solution and have pretty much memorized the variety of tools used to clean my teeth. You might say that the dentist chair is my home away from home.

You also might be curious as to why I make all these visits to the office recliner. Simply put, false choppers were way too common on my mother's side of the family. My dear mother and all my aunts had their teeth extracted at a very young age and false grinders were placed in their stead. I think my one sustaining grace for still having my teeth today, besides the dentist chair, is the fact that my father came from a line of beautiful, straight, pearly whites in his family and he still had them all except one when he passed through the pearly white gates of Heaven.

So you see, the dental hygienist is my friend because she keeps my choppers attached to my gums. Well, most of the time, until my hang tough attitude suddenly went south one morning and my visit to the dentist turned into a molar nightmare!

As I sat down she placed the paper bib around my neck and we started the usual gab session before she started jingling the tools. Then like clock work she handed me the protective glasses, these by the way, are so big they cover an area from the forehead to the upper lip. Then began the well rehearsed process of cleaning, scraping, polishing and flossing.

With my head down and slightly tilted to one side, she began cleaning front to back. Now, might I mention at this juncture of the story that all my Dentists and Hygienists through the years have remarked on how small my mouth is. I tell this to Bob on my return visits but he isn't so convinced! However, I bring up this professional knowledge because the truth is, the dental workers all have a struggle getting to the back of my mouth to work. And when they finally do reach their intended destination my gag reflexes kick in to full gear and like an animal with its collar cinched too tightly around its neck I have been known to sink my canines (okay, eyeteeth) into whatever obstruction is closing off my windpipe!

As the Hygienist wrestled her way past my tongue to my back molars she had to wiggle her tool, not to mention her body, for leverage to get the job done. *Just routine,* I remind myself as I lay with tilted head, sunglass shield and a hundred and some odd pounds over my head. But this is where my stress free visit took a nasty turn and ushered me into the molar nightmare.

The tool she was using, with all the force of pressure behind it, suddenly slipped with a scraping familiarity I had never experienced before. This force traveled across my gums at hurricane speed, so much so that my neck experienced a whiplash of sorts. If this wasn't concerning enough, my hygienist flew back in her chair with a look of panic and disbelief on her face.

Now at this breach of the story (I use the word breach because it means 'a gap where a break has occurred'), I realized that this was no ordinary visit. I sat straight up in my chair while she began rocking back and forth in hers while holding one hand tightly shut. Now panic set in on my face as I quickly tried to take a tongue count of my choppers.

Then she spoke while her hand remained tight fisted. "I can't believe it, I am so sorry." Hmm, I don't know about you, but those are not the kind of words I want to hear from the medical profession. Now it was my turn to speak. "Did you just yank out my tooth?" Slowly she began to uncurl her hand. Was that a molar in her hand? This is the first phase of shock. If it is a tooth, who might I ask, does it belong too? This second phase of shock is always denial. The third phase of shock? Please tell me this is just a bad dream!

But it was not a dream, it was a toothless reality and I was living it. Then she said something that made me want to hug her and cuff her at the same time. Hug her, because Mama Molar had not been uprooted from the only home she has ever known, but wanting to cuff her because of the extreme trauma she had just caused herself, not to mention yours truly here, when it was only a "crown" that she had removed.

I think it would have been easier on us both if she would have said, "Ha, well take a look at this. I Just popped a crown from your tooth, but no problem we will get that glued back in a jiffy and I will even toss in an extra toothbrush and floss for the minor inconvenience." Well, the Doc came in shortly after and that's exactly what he did and in just a few minutes all my grinders were back in business. And you will be happy to know that the hygienist and I both breathed a sigh of relief and parted with our usual warm goodbyes.

This experience reminded me that we all have probably had something yanked out of our lives at one time or another. Whether it is the sudden death of a loved one or a divorce, or maybe the loss of a friendship that was so dear to our hearts. Whatever the reason in those moments of unsettled peace, have you surrendered to the lie that no amount of glue could put your life back together? Some of you may have experienced a betrayal that knocked you down and took your very breath away, taking with it your security and trust.

May I encourage you with the good news that God is still in the crown making business. Not the crowns for our teeth of course but for our heads.

The Bible says in Psalms 103:4 that God redeems your life from the pit and crowns you with love and compassion. Life's unexpected losses and struggles can cause our crowns to become lopsided, off centered and unbalanced. Some of us perhaps were hit with such a sudden jolt that our crowns fell completely off our heads and shattered in a million pieces.

Listen dear one, when loss happens, God will fashion for us a new crown and after He has rescued us with His endless supply of love and compassion He will place that beautiful crown right back on our heads.

Chester - The World's Greatest Dog

Jennifer Knox

Romans 2:4 Or do you show contempt for the riches of his kindness, tolerance and patience, not realizing that God's kindness leads you toward repentance.

I knew my mom was completely gone the day that she called and told me that her new puppy, Chester, had excellent paw control! If you aren't sure what excellent paw control means, join the club. I'm pretty sure my mom was the first to coin the phrase, and also to bestow this honor upon her beloved Chester.

My mom had wanted a dog for quite some time, but it couldn't be just any dog, it had to be the right dog! The perfect dog! Well, my family was just the one to give her what she wanted. We had embarked on a journey to share the gift of life with our four children by breeding our two dogs. Once the puppies were of age, we finagled my mom into taking one of the puppies. She had wanted a female, but they were all claimed right away, so she was left with a little male. Since we had to wait until he was of age to fly (yes, they have a required puppy age for flights), we sent her daily pictures of her new little man. Already, I could tell it was going to be love at first sight.

The day that Chester made his arrival to Georgia to meet his new family, I was called by a very emotional mom who was holding her new baby … she was in love! My mom took an entire week off work to have special "Chester time." In that week, Chester was pampered, snuggled, played with, adored, loved, and trained. He quickly learned that this was going to be the life! It was not long into his new life in Georgia that he was given a soccer ball to play with. My mom would kick him the ball and he was indeed the world cup champion soccer dog, thus the phrase, "excellent paw control" was born.

A couple years had passed when we finally got to fly out as a family and see my mom, her husband and yes, the amazing Chester! We could hardly wait to be reunited with the little puppy we had seen come into the world, and watched grow up through volumes of photos and emails. My mom didn't exaggerate. He really was as beautiful as she had said. Chester was a handsome, hundred pound dog with beautiful blond fur and a tail that could effortlessly send a full cup of coffee soaring through the air, but that's a story for another time!

It wasn't long, though, before Chester "The World's Greatest Dog," would make a "bad boy" decision. I didn't actually know that Chester could do wrong, but sure enough when the front door opened, Chester went flying at top notch speed out the door and down the road! My mom went chasing after "The World's Most Perfect Dog" yelling, of all things, "CHESTER … CHEESE!!! CHEESE CHESTER, CHEESE!" At first I thought I wasn't hearing her properly, maybe she is saying, "Please, Chester, Please!" But no, it was indeed, "CHEESE!" That apparently is his punishment for running out of the front door. And what dog wouldn't learn not to run out the front door with such a horror awaiting them, the dreaded cheese! Our dear little, well, not so little Chester heard the words and quickly came back with tail wagging for his punishment. He was quickly given some fresh cheese from the refrigerator to learn his lesson! I was in awe. Was this the same mom that had disciplined me all my life? I don't ever recall being given cheese in response to going against the rules! But then, I wasn't "The World's Greatest Dog!"

This wouldn't be the last time we would see Chester make a mistake, though! My mom and her husband, Alan, hired a professional photographer to take family photos in their backyard. They have a picturesque backyard with an in-ground pool complete with waterfall. Everyone was dressed and ready for the pictures including Chester all clean, shiny and ready for yet another photo shoot. It was just about then that Chester decided it was time for a swim! Now, he is a beautiful dog, but let's all face it, a wet dog is not a pretty picture ... even if you are Chester!

My mom was shocked that Chester would jump in the pool without her permission! Apparently he knows to only go in the pool at their command, but this day he couldn't resist the cool refreshment of the pool. Without any warning he was soaked, swimming and happy! This was actually the first moment I saw my mom firm with Chester, the perfect dog. She quickly commanded him out of the water and scolded him saying, "Bad boy! Bad!" Then she looked at Alan in all seriousness and said, "You know what this means ... we're gonna need a fresh towel!" Alan was back in a flash with a fresh clean towel to rub down naughty, soaking wet Chester. He sat there patiently as my mom rubbed him down from head to paw with the fresh towel, all the while informing him that he did a bad thing. I could see the remorse on his face as he was massaged with the fluffy, fresh, clean towel. I wondered how long it would be before he decided he needed another cool dip followed by a nice rub down! His punishments were apparently fierce. I mean who wouldn't shudder at the thought of cheese and a long rub down!

The whole thing got me thinking about God. How often I have felt that my failures would be met with anger by a fierce God, yet instead I was lifted up out of my mess by anything but that. He has been a God of mercy, forgiveness and love. I can't count the times that I have deserved punishment, but received a word of tenderness and encouragement in its place. How true the scripture is when it says, "It's his kindness that leads us toward repentance." I pray that we will all hear the call of our Heavenly Father to come back home when we run away. He longs to hold us, not to harm us. And when He calls us back, He's got a whole lot better than cheese awaiting us!

The Chosen Ones

Margie McCready

Colossians 3:12 Therefore, as God's chosen people, holy and dearly loved, clothe yourselves with compassion, kindness, humility, gentleness and patience.

There she was standing at the back door. My 8 year old daughter, Corinne, only came to the back door when she was bringing something that she knew would never be welcome at the front door. Sure enough. I opened the door. She had clutched in her arms a scroungy looking cat. Its fur was going every direction. It was the homeliest cat I had ever seen. At first glance, it looked like someone had thrown three buckets of paint on this cat; black, orange and brown. The colors were all muddled together. I couldn't even see its eyes. Whoever the parents were of this particular cat, one thing was for certain; it was a bad combination. I rolled my eyes. She always knew the right thing to say. "Mom, I think he is starving to death," were her first words. I was stuck and I knew it. "Bring him in," I said. "We'll feed him and then you need to take him back where you found him." "Mom I can't," she wailed. "I found him hiding under a dirty log." My daughter had eyes like a hawk. He would have blended in completely in the forest. If there was a stray animal within a mile radius of our home she would find it, or should I say they would find her. Needless to say, the cat found a new place to call home; specifically 3025 Hancock Street. She named her Savannah, although I am sure it was a male. Not only was this cat sore on the eyes, he was allergic to fleas! I looked at the veterinarian like he had just grown another head. A cat allergic to fleas? How could that be possible? It sounded like an oxymoron. That was just one of the many challenges we had with this cat. They say cats have nine lives. Not this one. It was more like one hundred and nine. He was the first of many strays that graced our home. Corinne never wanted the pretty ones with pedigrees and no issues; she was always drawn to the "homeless and needy."

I look back now and I realize my daughter had a wonderful trait that we all need to have. It is called "compassion," and is desperately needed in our world today. There are many stray people all around us needing love and attention. Jesus was drawn to these very people – the outcasts of society that no one else wanted. He saw something in them that my daughter saw in those flea infested cats … … WORTH. It wasn't easy for me all those years, and all those cats. You see, I am allergic to cats! Doesn't the Lord have a great sense of humor? I survived the many ups and downs of pet ownership and learned valuable lessons watching Corinne tend and care for these unwanted critters.

Corinne is 32 now and just last week she stopped by for a visit. I couldn't believe the first words out of her mouth! "Mom, I have a new cat. I found it in the woods near our house. It was all skin and bones. I couldn't believe it was even alive. I am feeding it and I think it is going to make it. It is a beautiful tabby." I just looked at her and smiled. I silently thanked the Lord that I didn't need to go buy a new bottle of allergy pills. This cat would be living on Lindsey Lane.

I am grateful that I allowed my daughter to use the gift of compassion the Lord has given her. It has enriched her life and taught me the value of being sensitive and attentive to others less fortunate than myself. Hmmmm … sounds like someone else I know …

Favorite Things

Margie McCready

Malachi 3:17b … they will be my treasured possession.

I will never forget watching the movie 'The Sound of Music' as a young girl. It is a heart warming and true story depicting the lives of The Von Trapp Family Singers and the nanny who came to take care of them. It won 5 Academy Awards in 1965. My favorite scene in the entire movie is when the nanny, played by Julie Andrews, comforts the children one night during a storm. She sings to them one of the best loved songs in this musical, when she sings of her 'favorite things.'

All of us have our favorite things. Something that we prefer, that suits our liking and taste. It is what we favor and are partial towards. Sometimes they are not things at all, but people. My own dear mother had many favorite things. I know this because I clung to her apron strings for most of my childhood. I adored her. She loved the simple things in life. Without a doubt, on the top of my mother's list of favorite things, her children. Nothing ever came close. We were all specially loved, and we knew it. This was not an easy task for her, as she had 9 children. That is a lot of lives to nurture and love, but when it came to making someone to feel special and loved, my mother was an expert. She poured her life into her children.

I was number 7 in the line. I was also a very sickly child. I developed a severe case of whooping cough at 8 months old and nearly died. After that, I seemed to have a weak immune system and I was always sick with some ailment. My mother would rock me and sing to me for hours. Her voice comforted me. I never remember her telling me she was too busy, or tired, or she needed time alone. Never once. Just how special was I to my mother? I have a little keepsake box that I pull out every so often when I am feeling sad. In this box of treasures are all my little fingernails in envelopes as a baby. My mother saved them all. I've never opened them, but I can feel the little tiny clippings through the envelope. She wrote on the outside, 'Margie's Fingernails' and then how many months I was. I handle them very tenderly. I also have my first lock of hair in an envelope. It is not sealed and it is still very soft and very blonde. I have my baby book, which she took the time to write specific details in. I have all my birthday candles from my first birthday, all the way through my childhood. My first little pair of baby shoes are still perfectly tied, and my first dress is stained but oh-so beautiful. I have my first doll, a Raggedy Ann that looks like she has been beaten up a couple hundred times, and it is very obvious she had weathered many a childhood storm with me. Her little dress is stained with tears. I could go on and on, but I think you get my point. Without a doubt, I was my mother's favorite, along with Karen, Diane, Danny, Hector, John, Patty, Donald, and David. My mother knew a truth back then that I am just now learning, it is one that is forever etched in my heart. Of all the things that we possess on this earth, our children are the only things that we can take to Heaven with us. They are eternal. The rest we are leaving behind. All of it. What a sobering thought.

God has favorite things also. On the top of His list? You guessed it, His children! He loves each one of us. He delights in us! I know this personally. You see, every hair on my head is numbered. He loves me so much He can't take his eyes off of me. All of my tears are bottled in heaven. I am engraved on the palm of His hand. His thoughts of me outnumber the grains of sand on the seashore. I am never out of His sight, or out of His reach. He will go to any length to prove how deep His love for me really is. Even sending His own Son to die on a cross so that I could know Him personally and I can be forgiven.

Are you one of God's favorites? You can be. His invitation is open to anyone who will accept it … or should I say 'Him.' He stands at the door of your heart and knocks, but only you can open the door and let Him in. He is waiting … to shower you with His favor.

The Scarf

Jennifer Knox

> *Proverbs 17:22 A cheerful heart is good medicine, but a crushed spirit dries up the bones.*

Have you ever had a friend that just makes you laugh? I don't mean a chuckle here and there, I mean gut aching, tear falling, side splitting laugh! I have a dear friend who gets me laughing every time we're together. The funny thing about our friendship is that while we are having a laugh fest over our own mishaps, our husbands are usually ensconced in a deep theological discussion. For some reason that just makes the situation all the more funny to me. As we are discussing how funny it was that we had toilet paper stuck to our shoe at church (true story) our husbands are discussing the nature of God. It could make me feel shallow, but I've decided it is just a way to make my heart healthy. I consider it a replacement to walking on the treadmill. Some people work out … I laugh!

There was one day in particular that I have relived over and over. My friend and I were sitting on her couch, as we normally would, and our husbands were discussing the Bible, as they normally would, when she began to tell me about her most horrific experience. She and her husband were attending a Christian concert together. As they were walking from the parking lot to the event, she started noticing pressure forming near her … well … let's say her lower feminine region. The more they walked the more pressure she felt. Her mind started racing as to what it could be. She had heard that after having children, women have been known to have their uteruses drop right out of them! The more she thought about the possibility of her uterus falling out of her, the more she wondered what a person does when their uterus drops out of them in public! Do you pick it up and put it back in? How would you do that without anyone noticing?

As the pressure continued to build with each step, she finally couldn't take the suspense any longer and looked down to see what was going on … or falling out! To her surprise, it was her scarf! She had a long, knee length scarf on, and as she walked, the scarf had inconveniently made its way between her thighs, creating a wagging tail behind her. I'll never forget as she choked out the words, "My thighs ate my scarf!" I could not contain the laughter! I not only laughed the rest of that night with her, I laughed all night in my bed. I tried to contain it, but it only made the bed shake, waking my husband. When he asked what was so funny it sent me into a fit of laughter again. I actually had to cover my face with my pillow to muffle the laughter.

It has been years since the night my friend shared her "scarf" story with me and I still can find myself covering my face with my pillow to keep from waking my husband as I relive the visual of that scarf flopping side to side from the rear view. It reminds me of the verse in Proverbs 17:22 A cheerful heart is good medicine, but a crushed spirit dries up the bones.

It does feel good to laugh! But I have also known many days and even years of a crushed spirit. When the scripture says that "a crushed spirit dries up the bones" it is completely true. It can consume every drop of life and joy from our weary souls. By God's faithfulness, I have come out of that season and He truly has restored my joy, and brought life to my broken heart. There may be some of you that are reading this, and your spirit is crushed. If so, may I encourage you with the words found in Psalms 30:5

"Weeping may stay for the night, but rejoicing comes in the morning." I am praying that your joy, and your laughter will come again soon. The Lord loves you and is watching ever so carefully over you.

Living In The Palm Of His Hand

Margie McCready

Isaiah 49:16 See, I have engraved you on the palm of my hands.

I entered my daughter's room and there was a chill in the air, unlike any other I had felt before. I sat on the edge of her bed, and I knew, deep in my heart that she was dying. The thought was suffocating. She opened her eyes. I was staring death in the face and I knew it. I didn't like what I saw. "Mom ..." she whispered, "I can't do it anymore. I have to let go. I can't fight this." I instantly grabbed her. "No!" I said, "You can't give up! You have to live!" I began sobbing and praying and trying to will her to live. The deep, dark circles under her eyes were evident. She was frail and weak and barely breathing.

I went downstairs, put my head on the kitchen table, and cried uncontrollably. She was my miracle baby and the thought of losing her now, at the age of 20 was incomprehensible. You see my daughter had a twin that I lost early on during my pregnancy. The doctor only gave her a slim chance of surviving. Survive she did! She weighed 8 pounds 10 ounces and was perfect in every way … until now. She was diagnosed with thyroid cancer. Three surgeries in three weeks had left her weak and vulnerable, and very susceptible to pneumonia. It hit her full force and the doctors tried everything, but nothing was working. "We have done everything we can. She is now in God's hands."

It took a wrestling match with the Lord to show me that she really belonged to him and was in the palm of his hand. She always had been. I had tried to take ownership of her the night before I walked into her room, the day she was dying. I point blank told the Lord, "You cannot have her. She is mine. I won't let you take her." I cried and I cried and I cried until I could no longer cry and then I wrestled with God. In the end, we both know who won. I had to let her go. I had to surrender her and I had to tell the Lord, "She is yours Lord, you have every right to do with her what you want." I cried myself to sleep. I was broken and exhausted and empty. When I woke up the next morning I had a deep peace, the peace that passes all understanding. I thought of the scripture that says,

"God is in the heavens and does whatever he pleases." We all need to remember that. He is sovereign. He is in control. Because His love for us is so deep and limitless, we can trust His judgments. His ways are always right and always good.

My daughter's coughing brought me back to reality. I lifted my head from the table and went back upstairs. I surrendered her completely and let go of her. I placed her back in the palm of His hand where she belonged. I thanked the Lord for the privilege of allowing me to love her for 20 years. And then I said, "Your will be done." I meant it.

A miracle took place that day. That very afternoon, my daughter turned the corner. She lived! God spared her life. She is completely cancer free and healthy. For those who struggle in believing in miracles, I can honestly tell you from experience, that miracles are real. My daughter is visible truth. She truly is a walking miracle. Twice.

Slip And Slide With Hot Flashes

Patty Knox

Isaiah 12:3 With joy you will draw water from the wells of salvation.

To those who have experienced hot flashes, or the "vapors" as some like to call them, is like having lightning strike your body. Not just once but a million times over! It signals a heat wave from head to toe that radiates enough energy to run an electric car. I've heard menopausal women are now purchasing electric cars and fueling them with hot flashes. They always run on full tanks too as the Vapors are solar powered and give off energy all day and night.

Seriously here, these episodes of overheating are awful to experience and one never has any warning as to when they will occur. However, it is quite obvious when they do surface, as the face turns a flashing red color which signals to you and all people present that someone's internal thermostat is stuck on high!

I could not begin to tally the number of times I have been at the supermarket and had one of these "vapor episodes" only to find myself hot trotting it over to the nearest freezer section and practically climbing inside just to cool off. I'm sure my body heat has thawed out the frozen vegetables on several occasions.

I have thrown off covers so many times in bed at night that I now burn more calories sleeping than awake, while my poor hubby freezes from the high winds my sheets cause flapping back and forth!

Something, I realized, had to be done about these "night time vapors" so I decided to invest in silk sheets since they are cool to the touch, airy and light. I went to the store and splurged on a set that I thought would do the trick. But instead, I was the one tricked.

First night with these cool silk sheets proved to be a joke when our heels snagged across the bottom of the material. It was similar to strapping sandpaper on one's feet. Every time our feet moved Bob and I shredded the bottom of the sheets. This not only caused an annoyance but now I had to put socks on my feet and really upped the temperature in my body.

Oh, they were airy for sure. So airy that my pillow disappeared into thin air at night. These promising silk sheets were so slippery that our pillows slid to the floor when we turned over. Yikes! Those silk sheets were compounding my hot flash problem, not addressing it.

One particular morning I woke up and bent over my side of the bed to fetch my pillow off the floor and it was nowhere in sight. I looked over and noticed Bob's pillow was in its place and I was stumped! I then leaned over his side of the bed and there was my pillow! How did my pillow get all the way on the opposite side of the bed?

The mystery unfolded later that day when Bob informed me that when his pillow slid off the bed he just tugged on mine and when my head slid off my pillow with the cool, silk, airy and light pillowcase he snagged it instead of retrieving his own! That's when I threw those nightmare sheets and pillowcases right in the garbage. I went back to flapping covers all night and Bob continued to brave the high winds.

I have had enough slipping and sliding with hot flashes. I have decided to wait for the temperature to cool and call it good. Now, if I can just apply that same rule to my emotional hot flashes when I feel my temperature rising because I am upset about something. By simply waiting until the temperature gauge drops, I could keep my feelings from slipping and sliding all over the place too.

The Bible speaks about rivers of living water available to quench our thirst and since Jesus continually offers us cool refreshment from His well of salvation, I just need to remind myself daily that I can handle any kind of hot flash whether it be physical, emotional or spiritual as long as I have a tall glass of His life cooling water on hand.

Annie, Annie Are You Home

Margie McCready

Philippians 4:13 I can do all this through him who gives me strength.

I was working in a Christian daycare that was housed in our church. My supervisor informed me one morning that I would be getting two new children in my class. They were two year old twin boys. My first pregnancy had resulted in twins, so I figured I had some hands on experience that would be very helpful to me. My class was already close to capacity but I felt I could handle two more just fine. I anxiously awaited their arrival. When the door finally opened a little boy came flying by me, very excited and talking a million miles a minute. A typical little boy. My eyes were fixed on the door as I was waiting for his brother to come barging in also. Much to my surprise, a very tiny little boy whose legs didn't really bend all the way came slowly walking in. He walked like his legs were

After about a week, I noticed a pattern with his eating. For some reason his swallowing mechanism didn't operate correctly. Instead of his food going down his throat, it would go up and come out his nose. I had to make sure the pieces were very tiny and his food was very soft. Then one day it happened. He managed to steal a piece of string cheese from the little girl next to him. He took a huge bite before I could get it away from him. He knew he was in trouble so he swallowed it and began to choke! I was horrified as I watched his face turned red and the string cheese come out each nostril. It looked like spaghetti and was growing longer by the second. I managed to help him work through it, but as soon as my supervisor came in, I told her I couldn't do that again. Not only was it too stressful for me, I couldn't give my other kids the attention they needed, as I clearly had to focus most of my attention on him. She said she would take care of it. I was so relieved! It wasn't what I thought. She informed me the next day that she had signed me up for an industrial first aid course at our local hospital.

It wasn't just a regular first aid class; this one was grueling and very intense. It was three nights a week for eight weeks. It was a nightmare. It was the hardest class I have ever taken. One class particularly stands out in my mind. I was exhausted after working all day and I dragged myself to class. I didn't even have time to eat. I was ready to quit this class and my job. I was overwhelmed and daydreaming, until Annie came on the scene. The teacher carried Annie to the middle of the room and laid her on the floor. She was a very pretty blonde dummy that we were going to practice CPR on. I cringed. I felt like Annie. In fact, I could have played Annie that night. I felt like all the life had been sucked out of me, and I needed someone to breathe new life into me.

Now, every class has one person who is highly motivated and an overachiever. In our class, it was a man in his 30's named Jack. When it came time for Jack's turn, he ran to Annie and began talking to her like she was a real person. He was so energetic to help her and he kept yelling out very loudly, "Annie! Annie! Are you home? Annie! Annie!" He was vigorously pumping her chest. After a few minutes he finally looked at the teacher and said, "Well, the lights are on, but nobody's home." He had killed her. He had killed Annie. He got an F. I laughed so hard I nearly fell out of my chair! I aced the CPR class and successfully resuscitated Annie. That's when it hit me. If I can breathe new life into a dummy, then surely God can breathe new life into me. I just need to trust him. My whole perspective changed. That night, I gave my heavy load to Jesus. I surrendered it and let it go. The heaviness lifted and I passed the course with flying colors. I gained a tremendous amount of medical knowledge and I had a new confidence that I was now trained to handle any emergency situation that popped up. Even choking.

When I find myself in challenging times now, and I begin to feel overwhelmed, I just think of Annie and I know that there is hope for me. No matter what.

Laser Tag

Jennifer Knox

1 Peter 5:8 Be alert and of sober mind. Your enemy the devil prowls around like a roaring lion looking for someone to devour.

Has it ever amazed you how two siblings can be raised by the same parents, have the same upbringing and turn out completely opposite? That is me and my sister, April. She is four years older than me, and we couldn't be any more different from each other. My sister is a nature lover, I am a coffee lover. She loves activity, I love tranquility. She loves planning, I love spontaneity. What we do have in common is we love spending time together. We don't get to see each other often, being that we live in different states, but when we do, it's a blast!

This past year we jumped on the chance for a family reunion to celebrate my fortieth birthday and my daughter's sixteenth. My sister arrived with her three children for the big celebration. It is always such a treat to see how my nieces and my nephew are growing.

As I mentioned earlier, my sister loves activities. Her idea of fun is a marathon on top of a mountain range (she really has done this … twice!). My idea of fun would be to get a good cup of coffee and talk about what it's like to run a marathon on top of a mountain range. So as we were pondering what to do while she and the kids were in town visiting us, she came up with the idea to play laser tag. I was less than amped up about the prospect of running around in the dark and shooting lasers at strangers, but not wanting to be a "dudder" I agreed to go.

Before I knew what was happening, we were putting on our gear and pulling out our lasers. The doors to the two story room opened and everyone took off into the music pumping, dark, glowing, smoke machine filled room. I just stood there staring at the "marshall" (that's the person we go to in case of an emergency). There was nobody around us, just me and the marshall, everyone else had taken off. I stood there afraid to leave the safety of my now best friend Mr. Marshall. I decided I would just stay close to him until the game was over. As a couple minutes passed I ventured a few feet away from my safety zone and caught a glimpse of my twelve year old nephew, Jacob. It was at that moment that the strangest thing happened, I turned into laser tag G.I. Joe! I was immediately in hot pursuit of him. As I got a bead on his target I pulled the trigger and BAM ... I got him! I was so delighted at my successful hit that I threw my hands up in victory and cheered for myself! It was all over from there. The absolute thrill I received from getting my twelve year old nephew was an adrenaline high! Now it was time to hunt down my ten year old niece, Sabrina!

I snuck around the building like a pro, hunkering down in dark places and popping out in time to get whoever was within target reach. Finally I found my niece and chased her around the compound getting her ten times! Oh, what a thrill! My last challenge, my six year old niece, Courtney! Out of the corner of my eye I saw her darting around a wall with my sister close behind her. I ducked around the corner until I could sneak up on her and BAM, I got her too! Oh the delight! I was tagging my little nieces and nephew and it was fabulous. I was relentless in my pursuit and laughing so hard I had tears pouring down my cheeks. I was made for this! I am Laser Tag Queen!

Then the siren sounded and the game was over. As the results from the game were handed out, I was eager to see if I had beaten anyone. Sure enough, I had taken down my ten and six year old nieces! Yah! Complete domination! Unfortunately my son and my nephew had beaten me … but there was still game two to play!

As I was laying in my bed that night I was thinking how fun the entire evening had been. Who would have thought that laser tag could be so much fun? I was already planning my strategy for our next round. I could wear darker clothes, I could hunker down lower, I could move a little faster … then I could pounce on my opponents! Then it hit me, this is how Satan is with us. The Bible says in 1 Peter 5:8 "Be alert and of sober mind. Your enemy the devil prowls around like a roaring lion looking for someone to devour." We can be tempted to live life as if there is no enemy out to get us, but that leaves us open to his attacks. The Lord warned us that we really do have an enemy who is not looking to shoot us with a laser beam, but he is out to completely destroy us! I have found the best way to be alert, is to keep my head in the game. I do that by staying in the Word of God and keeping my heart set on the things of God. Thankfully our God is stronger than our enemy, but we must continually obey the Lord when He gives us directives on how to avoid the traps the enemy has set for us. This life is no laser tag game, but praise the Lord we have God on our side!

Flee The Evil Desires Of Youth - And The Urge To Tan

Jennifer Knox

2 Timothy 2:22 Flee the evil desires of youth and pursue righteousness, faith, love and peace, along with those who call on the Lord out of a pure heart.

Forty snuck up on me without me looking. Last I checked I was twenty-something, now I'm forty! How did that happen? I still feel twenty-something, but my face is screaming forty-something. Actually, I was excited to turn forty, it seems so refined and mature. My entire family was going to come out to celebrate my birthday, and that only added to my excitement over the monumental day. On the whole, forty has been fabulous, although it's only been three months, but I can't say it's been without its glitches.

Just twenty-four short days after turning forty I had a doctors appointment to look at a spot on my arm. I noticed it forming several months prior, but tried to convince myself it was just another "age spot." To be honest I don't mind age spots, they actually somewhat fascinate me. When I look at my hands it always seems strange that they are mine, they look just like my grandmother's. That to me is a good thing, I adored my grandmother. However, the spots on my face, those aren't so endearing. I've decided I could do without the age spots on my face, but they don't seem to listen to my refusal to receive them … they just keep coming.

Anyway, back to the spot on my arm. One day while I was with my husband he grabbed my arm and looked intently at it. I knew what he was thinking because I had been thinking the same thing for months. He dropped my arm back down to my side and said flatly, "get that looked at, I think it's cancer." Ughhh, exactly what I had been trying to avoid, but now I had to deal with it. I wasn't too concerned, because I had already been my own internet doctor for the past couple months researching skin cancer. If it was cancer, it was not the serious kind, but would definitely need to be removed.

That brings me to the doctor appointment I had mentioned earlier. As I sat there she quickly assessed that the spot needed to be removed and have a biopsy ran on it. It was also decided that since I was now forty, I should have an all over check for any other abnormalities. I love the word "abnormality" because after my check-up I realized there is nothing normal about me. The process was shocking. As my doctor checked everything from my scalp, to my face, to my fingernails and all the way down to my toes, she never once stopped dictating to the nurse what she was finding. As she looked me over, the nurse's fingers were flying on the keyboard, documenting all my "abnormalities." Since I didn't recognize a single word that was spoken, I just laid there in utter astonishment at the foreign language the two were speaking about my skin conditions.

The conversation sounded something like this, "I see several idiopathic guttate hypomelanosis, I see several ephelis, I see lentigines, these are distinguished from ephelis based on the proliferation of melanocytes, I see several leukonychia, I see scarring, I see stretch marks (yes, I've had four kids, but they didn't seem interested in my explanations), she even went down and said I had calluses on the tops of my toes which are not normal. When we finished the exam, and I had recovered from the shame of it all, she looked straight at me and said, "Bottom line, no more sun for you!"

I wanted to say back to her, "Really, why? … Shouldn't we add a few more ephelis, lentigines and idiopathic guttates to my skin? I've grown so attached to them!" I decided against that and continued to listen as she warned me of the dangers the sun could cause me. I am apparently a higher-risk individual for skin cancer because of my skin type (I think I'm abnormal type). So, this means no more sun for me, which is sad because the sun is one of my best friends. I love the sun and the sun loves me … just my skin doesn't and it's causing me all this trouble!

This all seemed fine and dandy until recently when our family decided to go to Florida for ten days. I was already starting to fantasize about lounging by the pool basking in the sun, bronzing my freckled skin, when it hit me, I can't be in the sun! I can't even tan my white legs before we go! The horror! White legs in a tropical location! I immediately sent my mind searching for excuses for one more time in the sun, but the doctor's warnings kept ringing in my ears, "No more sun!"

As I pondered whether I would heed the doctor's warnings or indulge in one last sun soaking experience, I thought of the verse in 2 Timothy 2:22 "Flee the evil desires of youth and pursue righteousness, faith, love and peace, along with those who call on the Lord out of a pure heart." It was time for me to flee the evil desires of my youthful tan self, and choose the way of wisdom and white legs. As much as I hated the prospect, I knew it was the right thing to do. Isn't that just like our lives with the Lord though? We are told to flee the evil desires of youth, and to pursue righteousness, faith, love and peace. I started to ponder if I was doing what this scripture asked. Just like the doctor gave me the truth, I had a choice to follow her advice or not. In the same way, we have the choice to obey The Word of God, or to ignore it. The great thing about God is He knows best! If He asks something of us, we can know it is going to work for our good. So, being older and wiser, I have chosen to listen to my doctor and buy the sun-screen, visor, parka, large straw hat (you get the picture); and also to make sure that I am listening to the voice of God leading me in the way to go.

I've decided I like forty. I like fleeing the things that once brought me down and led to emptiness. I like the life of pursuing things that will bring life to me and to others. I like growing in wisdom and understanding. I like age spots on my face ... well, maybe I don't like that part, but I do like the life God has for me as I choose to obey His ways!

Yikes, What's Up With The Ites

Patty Knox

> *Psalms 74:2 Remember the nation you purchased long ago, the people of your inheritance.*

Is it just me or have you also noticed all the "ites" attached to the Old Testament clans? After peering closer I discovered there is every name of "ites" imaginable. Allow me to toss a few names your way. Hey, let's start from A and see if we can name clans all the way to Z.

Ready? Amalekites, Bekerites, Cushites, Danites, Erites, Gibeonites, Hamites, Israelites, Jakinites, Kohalites, Levites, Moabites, Nazarites, Oznites, Perezites, Rubenites, Shemites, Temanites, Uzzelites, and Zerahites. Whew! Who knew? And that is just the tip of the iceberg on all the "ites" mentioned in the Bible, as there are double and triple in most of the letters. In fact, my family's tribe would fall under the letter K, the "Knoxites" sounds like a noxious weed killer doesn't it? The only alphabet letters that I could not find a clan for were F, Q, and V but who knows, I'm sure Moses used those letters more than a few times when he was trying to herd the Israelites out in the desert for forty years. Faithlessites, Quarrelsomeites, and maybe even Venomites!

All this triggered my curiosity on how many "ites" we may be familiar with in our culture today. Just off the top of my head I came up with Socialites, Campsites, Websites, Megabites, Termites, Parasites, Bugbites, Dogbites, Underbites and Overbites! Go ahead toss in your own "ites" here.

I'm beginning to see that all this "ite" stuff may be linked to a generational glue passed down to link us all together in one form or another. I also discovered that in the Old Testament every "ite" referred to a place, group or family unit.

Most of us are familiar with the Israelites of the bible who were chosen by God to be His special people, not because they were better or smarter than other clans because the word paints an entirely different picture of these "ites". One that displays a stubborn, stiff necked and rebellious people. I remember asking my husband Bob once why he thought God would have ever chosen such a motley bunch of buffoons anyway.

And without missing a beat he replied "to show us what we are like" ... ... Ye-ikes for all of us "ites!"

The Israelites were forever running from God to other gods in search of acceptance, happiness and security but this only led to disappointment, hardship and captivity. And the same is true for us today. When we choose to leave our heavenly father's presence or have never known it, we are left strangers looking for a place to feel validated, recognized, and acknowledged.

Take for instance the "Moneyites" that dwell among us today. This tribe dwells in the mansions of false security believing that money can buy security and fulfillment, but should the stock market fail and the money suddenly disappear, they are left displaced, disillusioned and dissatisfied. Or what about the "Amnesiaites?" This clan either forgot who they belong to or have never been told who they really are. These "ites" have absolutely no clue to their true state of identity and forever look to Hollywood, magazines and this present culture to tell them what they need to achieve or look like to be accepted. So hungry for belonging the "Amnesiaites" lick up the lies like a tot licking a triple scoop ice cream cone. But instead of being satisfied and content, they are left empty and scurry to another voice that will point them to finding out who they are and where they fit.

We all belonged to the "Lostites" tribe before we found Christ and learned what our purpose, significance and true identity looks like. Again the bible tells us that We have all like sheep gone astray looking for that green pasture that will meet all our needs. We knowingly or unknowingly have mapped out and traveled to destinations looking for a place to fit in and call home. To be loved, valued and noticed, cherished and needed. These are all God given needs but the problem comes in to play when we try to meet them ourselves rather than allowing our creator, who knows exactly where we fit in, to meet those needs.

Jesus paid a very high premium to purchase our true identity. He not only mapped out the directions to get there through His word, He also paved the way to our new address which has "whosoever will may come" over the doorway! The red color over the doorstop assures all security on the inside, Jesus welcomes all travelers to stop in and let Him tell you where you really belong, and that is home with Him in His Father's house!

Johnny's Socks

Margie McCready

Matthew 8:11 I say to you that many will come from the east and the west, and will take their places at the feast with Abraham, Isaac and Jacob in the kingdom of heaven.

My dad was in the last few months of his life. He had been diagnosed with cancer and it had no intention of going away. As hard as it was for me, I knew I had to accept it. My dad and I had become very close in the last few years since my mother had passed away. I began taking care of him on a weekly basis and doing all of his shopping, as it had become very difficult for him to walk. During one of the many trips to see his doctor, he caught me off guard. As we were passing by the mortuary he piped up and said, "Well, pretty soon I'll be lying in there." Startled I replied, "Dad, don't say that!" He looked over at me nonchalantly and said, "Well it's the truth, ya know."

I tried to change the subject, as I had no desire to continue that conversation. My dad was sharp as a tack and the attempt failed. "Now listen." He chimed in, "You make sure when I'm buried that I'm wearing Johnny's socks." I stared at him with a deer in the headlights look. "What, Dad?" He then proceeded to tell me about these special socks that my brother John had given him a few years earlier for father's day. "They came in a 3-pack but I saved one pair in my top drawer. You'll see it there." I wanted to burst into tears.

It didn't stop there. He continued on to make sure I understood that he wasn't to be buried in any fancy duds. "Make sure I have on my overalls and my suspenders. I don't want to be wearing anything unfamiliar and uncomfortable." I was really struggling at this point to keep it together. I was so relieved when we arrived at our destination and our conversation ended. I was totally unprepared for how much I was going to miss my dad. I prayed when I exited the car that the Lord would help me focus on what was happening at the moment. This was not the time to fall apart.

A few weeks later, my dad passed away. I opened his top drawer, and true to his word, lay the new pair of Johnny's socks. This time, I did burst into tears. I allowed myself the space to grieve ... really grieve. There was no holding back the sobs now.

My sister Patty and I went to Dad's house a few days later to get his things for his burial. We didn't choose his best clothes, we picked his favorites; the tattered overalls that he loved, his red suspenders, his favorite shirt, his cap that he always wore when he left the house, and most importantly, Johnny's socks. We were leaving the house when I remembered his well-worn slippers and went running back in. There they were, lying next to the wood stove, covered in dog hair. They were usually toasty warm. Not this time. My dad had made his last fire.

I was reminded of Johnny's socks just last week when I had my grandson Cash over. I was taking Cash and his cousin Elijah to the park when I realized Cash needed warmer socks. Grandpa Mark was home for lunch and picked the smallest pair of socks out of his top drawer and put them on Cash. We spent the afternoon at the park, and the socks held up just fine. Arriving back at the house, the boys took off their shoes and went to the kitchen table for a snack. It was now 6 o'clock and my daughters would be arriving to scoop up the boys. I told Cash to put on his shoes. He looked down at his feet and said, "Granny, do you think Grandpa would mind if I kept his socks? I really like them, they are special." My mind instantly flashed back to Johnny's socks. I was so touched that I couldn't speak for a few seconds. "Of course you can keep Grandpa's socks." I said. I watched him pull them up so they would fit better in his shoes. I then thought of my dad wearing Johnny's socks and how for some reason they comforted him. I was deeply comforted.

Someday I will finish my journey on this earth and I will draw near to Heaven's gate. One of the first things I plan to do when I get to Heaven is look at my dad's feet. There's a good chance he'll be wearing … Johnny's socks.

Fearfully And Wonderfully Made?

Patty Knox

Psalms 139:14 I praise you because I am fearfully and wonderfully made.

I always wondered about the fearful part of being wonderfully made, until my physical body hit menopause and beyond. I've watched as time has marched across my face and left wrinkles in its aftermath, and then moved all the way down to my toes wanting to cross in every direction possible. I've experienced turkey neck syndrome, droop chest disorder, aged slouch infirmity, slump shoulder affliction, restricted hearing loss, extra chin hair growth and just about everything else that I deemed fearful when one ages. But nothing prepared me for the malady that began to appear on my body this last year.

I thought my body had pretty much cycled through the timeworn stages now that I was over 60.

Thought I had the fearful part of being wonderfully made over, but that theory proved false when my skin had a collision with something else in my body and the impact from it produced bumps, weird stretchy bumps. The medical profession calls them skin tags. I call them unnecessary!

Really? Like my body doesn't already wear the signs of aging and now I must don skin tags all over my frame? I guess one could make a game out of them by connecting the dots, or play skin tag you're it. Now, not only are these outgrowths annoying, but they seem to take on a journey of their own by popping up in the oddest places. Can I get an amen from the skin tag society? … I heard that amen!

I see no possible function in these skin imperfections other than to fulfill the scripture of being fearfully made. Or so I thought until I discovered what the Lord meant by being fearfully and wonderfully made.

In the original Hebrew text, the word 'fearfully' means: with great reverence and heartfelt interest and respect. The word 'wonderfully' means: unique, set apart, uniquely marvelous. According to the scriptures that is telling us all that we are a masterpiece of God's choosing. Persons with a divine purpose and destiny and worth.

No one else knows us at the most intimate level. We can become so preoccupied on imperfections that no one else notices. Too short, too tall, too heavy, too thin. For some of us it might not be physical dissatisfaction but the fear of not being smart enough or outgoing enough.

I am realizing now that true love and acceptance does not come by somehow changing our bodies or circumstances, but comes from the assurance that when God created us He made us exactly the way He intended to; our size, color of hair, eyes and skin.

I'm also beginning to see the value of my body from God's perspective (yes, chin hairs and skin tags included) and it is inestimable which means; beyond measure, worth of all human life from the womb to the final breath of human life. So the next time we look in the mirror and want to focus on our imperfections, let's try to focus on the truth that not only have we been fearfully and awesomely made, but we have also been made in God's image and frankly God don't make junk! Who knows, maybe even a skin tag has a purpose.

There's Cold Water On My Knee

Jennifer Knox

Proverbs 19:11b … it is to one's glory to overlook an offense.

I'm not sure how long it'd been happening, but I know it had to have been for several months before I finally recognized it. What was it? Cold water on my knee! Yup, multiple times everyday I found myself brushing off my left knee thinking there was cold water on it. Each time I spontaneously went for the wet spot, I noticed there was nothing there. I hadn't given it much thought until one particular day it was more noticeable. I knelt down to get some laundry and thought to myself, "Oh man! I just knelt in a puddle of water!" When I stood up to look, my pants were dry, no water on my knee at all! Then I started thinking back to the past several months and how I was always thinking there was water on my left knee.

Immediately my mind started racing to what disease I might have! I have a tendency to overreact. I had to have proof of my illness, as I was now convinced I had. I went straight to the authority on the matter … google! My hands were trembling as I tried to prepare myself for the diagnosis. Within moments I found the answer to my question … I was part of a community of "imaginary water feelers!" Yes, I belonged to this unique group. We were united in our cold water sensations. I spent hours reading the blogs of my new companions. Some experienced cold water sensations in their arms, elbows, hands, legs, but I really felt connected to the ones who felt it in their left knee. The mystery was solved, it wasn't water at all, but just the nerves sending my brain a faulty message.

After my diagnosis, I was fascinated by my imaginary cold water knee. It actually reminded me of offenses that I've had with others, or that they have had with me. I've been offended that people haven't got back to my emails, only to discover that they never got my email in the first place. Or hurt that someone didn't wave back at me, only to discover they hadn't seen me waving. It can also go the other way where people are offended at me. Being a pastor's wife, I've had several people approach me with an offense towards me, for things I didn't know anything about. Can't we all 'fess up to faulty accusations against someone? It's just like my brain saying there is water on my knee, when really there is nothing there. Our hearts can lay claim to something that isn't really there. Proverbs 19:11b says, "it is to one's glory to overlook an offense."

I remember one time I was greatly offended that my boyfriend (happy to state he's now my husband) was talking to other girls and completely ignoring me! In middle school, this is a major crisis! (Quick disclaimer, being much older and slightly wiser, I do not recommend middle schoolers having boyfriends!) Back to our story ... to make matters worse, it was one of the last days we would spend together before I had to move away. My parents had separated and my mom moved to Georgia. Due to their separation, I was leaving Seattle as well as my friends and boyfriend (the one I shouldn't have had because I was in middle school). It was an incredibly difficult time in my life and my boyfriend/husband was only aiding to the hurt by talking to other girls! Well, come to find out, they were planning a surprise going away party for me! Man, did I feel bad about how I had treated him when I found out the truth of the situation. I had taken offense over something that wasn't even there.

Sometimes we create offenses, and sometimes the offense is real. Either way, it is to our glory to overlook it. I'm so thankful that Jesus never holds my actions against me. Instead, He chooses to forgive me, overlook the offense, and love me. So the next time we reach down to wipe cold water off our knee (aka: feel an offense coming on) let's take the example of Jesus and choose to overlook the offense and hand out some love.

Forgiveness

Margie McCready

Matthew 6:15 But if you do not forgive others their sins, your Father will not forgive your sins.

It was 2009. I was standing next to my dad's bed in the emergency room. We had been there for hours, but still no word. There was a deafening silence hanging in the room. My dad was the first to break it. "Well Marge, I think this is the beginning of the end." A million thoughts swirled through my head. I couldn't process his words. You see, all growing up I didn't have a relationship with my dad. I so desperately wanted to be loved and accepted as his child, but it never happened. I lived through years of belittling and rejection. I tried so hard to be the best at everything to make him love me and be proud of me, but it never worked. What I didn't understand as a child, was that it wasn't me. I wasn't the problem. It was him. I finally resorted to avoiding him at all costs. It's like the dog that keeps biting you every time you reach out to pet him. After a while you finally stop.

In 2001, my sister Patty and I drove to the family home to bring birthday gifts to both my dad and mom. What we were not aware of was that my dad had driven my mom to a hospital that very morning, as she was very ill. She did not return home with him. He was very distraught and angry with us. He blamed us. "Why didn't you do something to help her?! Why didn't you fix her?!" He screamed at us. We were both shocked. We tried to reason with him. "You can't fix old age," I said to him, "Her body is tired and she worked hard her whole life." My mother had birthed nine children and raised them in a very unpleasant and hostile environment. Nothing we said convinced him. He went into a rage and threw us both out of the house. He said things I will not print on paper, let alone say to another living soul. He told us never to come back. He said he had never wanted us. We were devastated. We drove an hour to the hospital where he had taken our mother. We needed to see her. Little did we know, it was the last time we would ever see her again, as she died a few weeks later. A part of me died the day my mother passed away. I can't explain it. She had been my lifeline all of my life. She had tried to compensate for the negative effects of my father. And she had paid for it many a time.

I closed my heart to my father. I told my children never to speak of him around me again, and that when he died, I would not be at his funeral. I was so wounded and crushed. I told myself that I was justified in my feelings, although I knew in my heart that I was 100% wrong. I did not see my dad for 5 years, and during that time, the Lord was putting His finger on that open wound in my heart. I tried to ignore it, but it was robbing me of peace. I knew I had to forgive him. I didn't want to. Forgiveness is hard sometimes. I prayed for him every single morning and asked the Lord to help me forgive him. God did a miracle in my heart. A short time later God told me to "go." He said to me, "It is time." After 5 years of silence, God was opening the door for me to re-enter my father's life. It was one of the hardest things I have ever done. As I was driving to his house, the Lord said to me, very clearly, "Trust me."

For 3 years I helped take care of my dad. His health had deteriorated to the point where he could barely walk and could no longer drive. I took him to doctor appointments, did all of his shopping, and on Fridays cooked meals at his house that he could eat all week. And I prayed a lot. And I prayed even more. My dad's heart began to soften. He began opening up.

He started reading his Bible, and started watching Joyce Meyers on TV. It wasn't long after that, that he accepted the Lord. It was a miracle. The transformation was unbelievable. He was not the same person. He apologized for all those years of abuse. For 3 years, we had a real father-daughter relationship. He became one of my best friends. I can honestly say I loved him. It was genuine and real, and after 53 years I finally had a relationship with my dad that I only dreamed of. I was on top of the world.

He coughed and it brought me back to reality. I couldn't imagine losing him now. I couldn't even speak. My eyes filled with tears and he grabbed my hand, "It's going to be alright."

That fateful day in the ER truly was, "the beginning of the end." My dad died three months later. It was three of the most precious months of my life. It was gruesome, heart wrenching, and very hard to watch him die, but I wouldn't trade those times for the world. You see, I got to usher him into Heaven.

I learned a very valuable truth from the life of my mother, one that will be forever cemented in my heart. That truth is 'love is stronger than hate.' What a wonderful surprise for my mother to see my father come through Heaven's gates. He would have been the last person she would have expected to see.

Betty, Betty, This Way Betty

Patty Knox

Isaiah 30:21 Whether you turn to the right or to the left, your ears will hear a voice behind you, saying, "This is the way; walk in it."

Sitting in a hospital room for days with a precious loved one, my sister Margie and I had memorized every detail of the room itself. Late one afternoon we decided to turn our chairs toward the door in hopes of catching some new scenery. Little did we know, we were about to watch a live movie and before it was over, our only regret was that we didn't have popcorn during the matinee.

After watching several nurses, doctors and staff members breeze up and down the hallway the real drama, or should I say comedy, began when a tiny older woman shuffled next to our room decked out in all the usual hospital garb, from the backless gown to the sock slippers. She paused at our doorway long enough to sport a mischievous smile and then continued to meander down the hall.

"Betty, Betty," called a voice from the opposite end of the hallway from where Betty was headed. As the voice raced by our room, we saw that it belonged to a nurse. Seconds later she was leading Betty back up the hall exclaiming "this way Betty." Well, this scene played out several more times with Betty moving faster each time she escaped from her room. Her parade down the hall went from a shuffle, to a sprint and then a fast trot as she hotfooted it by our doorway, only to be retrieved by staff members, nurses, doctors, counselors, and even the cleaning ladies escorted her back up the hallway, and all delivering the same message, "Betty, Betty, this way Betty."

I think somewhere around the third lap of Betty's shenanigans, Margie and myself were cheering her on like an athlete running in a race. Not only was she adorable, but each time she scurried by our room, I noticed her bathrobe belt coming a tad bit loose and her gown shifting. If little Betty kept up this hurried pace and lost that robe, this movie was about to go from a G rated film to an R!

Oh! How we enjoyed seeing and hearing, "Betty, Betty, this way Betty!" But like all good flicks that come to an end, the action stopped, and though we hoped for an encore we never saw little Betty again.

That evening as we proceeded down the corridor to leave, we couldn't help but notice paper plates plastered to the walls with arrows and Betty's name written on them in bold black letters. Curious, and since we were headed in the same direction anyway, we followed the arrows. We passed several plates with Betty's name all pointing south up the hallway. This led us past several doorways. Then we noticed a sudden change in direction and now on the hospital wall was a taped paper plate with Betty's name alongside a huge arrow pointing north in the opposite direction! We were a bit confused at the sudden turn-around until we spotted a plate with Betty's name suddenly swerving our eyes west. As we followed this arrow, we came upon one last paper plate stuck to a hospital room door with Betty's name written in brazen capital letters! "BETTY." Margie and I now understood the reasoning behind the paper plate map, for we had reached Betty's intended destination. And since we didn't see any sign of Betty now, the paper plate map must have fulfilled its intended purpose. Mission accomplished! Betty was headed in the right direction, and the whole nurses station was breathing a sigh of relief.

I am still humored when I think about Betty's wanderings and the paper plate road map that helped to steer her in the right direction. And sometimes I even find myself blurting out loud, "Betty, Betty, this way Betty."

I wonder how many of us are a lot more like Betty than we would care to admit. The Lord has placed us on a path going in one direction and before we know it we have become side tracked and find ourselves going down unnecessary paths. How do we become sidetracked? It usually starts out as a distraction of some sort. It comes when we take our focus off of Jesus and His word and set our compass toward ourselves and our circumstances to guide us. The problem with looking to ourselves to navigate through our circumstances, is that when we face hard times, we will not only look for the quickest path out of our problems (believe me when I say I've taken this path more than a few times) but we can also become discouraged and focus on the rocks in front of us instead of the road ahead of us. Like Betty, we can lose our sense of direction and though we expend our energy walking, we are heading anywhere, everywhere and nowhere at the same time.

Thank goodness however, that we have a heavenly doctor who calls to us when He sees us heading in the wrong direction. I stand amazed and humbled by the knowledge that Jesus is willing to come after us as many times as it takes to gently guide us back to the pathway that leads to our intended destination. Might I add also, that I am grateful to know that His eyes are on us continually (Good thing, or like Betty, who knows where we would all end up, huh?). Now we know why the bible states that God never sleeps nor slumbers. He can't afford to!

I was truly moved by the fact that the nurses called Betty by her name each time they gently led her back to her room. She wasn't just a patient, she had an identity also. And I am moved still by the realization that the Lord knows our names and every other detail of our lives. He knows all the reasons, choices, and the circumstances that lead us to choose wayward paths. Plus we can all celebrate in the realization that our heavenly Father has an endless supply of paper plates with our names written on them, pointing us back like Betty, toward the intended direction for our journey.

Isaiah summed it up perfectly when he said, "whether you turn right or left you will hear a voice behind you, saying this is the way!" … … It worked for Betty and it will work for us too. Go ahead, insert your name instead of sweet little Betty's and speak it out. I'll go first … "Patty, Patty, this way Patty!"

The Broken Toe

Margie McCready

1 Corinthians 12:25-26 There should be no division in the body, but that its parts should have equal concern for each other. If one part suffers, every part suffers with it; if one part is honored, every part rejoices with it.

I woke up to my daughter Hillary crying. I didn't want to get up. I was tired, very tired. My life had seemed to spiral into a state of monotony. Every day seemed the same. I was looking for something different, some variety in my life. I needed some excitement. I felt like I was in a rut and the repetition was wearing me out. I also felt very unimportant. Shouldn't I be doing more? I thought. Mothering five children consumed all of my time.

My daughter's crying had stopped, and now she was calling out at a breakneck speed, "Mama! Mama! Mama! Mama!" I loved her little voice. I scooped her up and carried her downstairs. I then deposited her into her highchair and pulled it in close to the table, a little too close. I sat down next to her and began feeding her the oatmeal she loved. Then it happened. It happened so fast that I barely had time to react. She took her tiny little foot and put it on the sturdy leg of the kitchen table and pushed back. To my horror, she suddenly started falling over backwards! In a reflex action I jumped up to grab the highchair but misjudged where the table leg was. It just so happens that I forgot to put my slippers on that morning. I slammed my foot into the table leg with brute force. The pain was searing. I managed to stabilize the highchair but as soon as I had it on level ground, I found myself rolling on the floor, cradling my right foot and yelling at the top of my lungs. My yelling, in turn, made my daughter burst into tears. She was scared to death. She had never seen her mommy rolling on the floor screaming. I looked at my baby toe; it was the size of a small sausage and clearly broken. I tried to stand on my foot with little success. It was too painful. I managed to crawl to the phone and call my husband. "I need to go to the doctor!"

The doctor looked at me point blank. "There is nothing we can do for a broken toe." He said "It just has to heal on its own. It can take up to eight weeks."

I thought he was joking. I remember thinking to myself 'That is ridiculous. It is a small little toe. How important could that be?' I was wrong … dead wrong. The Lord showed me over the next eight weeks just how valuable a small toe is. I could hardly walk. I hobbled for weeks and I couldn't wear a shoe on that foot. It was far too painful. I had to wear an ugly brown slipper everywhere I went, which included: Church, the grocery store, graduation, a wedding, literally EVERYWHERE. I was humiliated. Here I was, entering a room with a shiny black heel on my left foot and an ugly brown slipper on my right foot … a very cushioned, flat, ugly brown slipper. And to make matters worse, I dipped to the right with every step I took, which made it even more noticeable. At the time, it was hard to see that this accident was actually good for me. I learned a very valuable lesson. Never despise the small things. The Lord showed me my ministry at that time was taking care of my five precious little ones. That was my calling. My whole perspective changed.

My toe took a lot longer than eight weeks to heal. It was a very bad break, but the Lord's timing is perfect, and He knows EXACTLY what we need. Now whenever I am feeling small and insignificant, I just look at my baby toe and remember. The Bible says we are all members of the same body and we need each other. One part is just as important as the other. Wherever the Lord has placed you in the body of Christ, just be. And thrive, and function, and grow. Just be what the Lord has called you to be. Within a few years I had more opportunities for ministry than I could have ever imagined, and the timing was right. He is the Potter and we are the clay. He will mold us into vessels fit for His kingdom.

3-D

Jennifer Knox

> *1 Corinthians 13:12 For now we see only a reflection as in a mirror; then we shall see face to face.*

I've always wanted glasses. Glasses are cool. Glasses make you smart. Glasses make you popular. At least those were my feelings on the matter. My earliest memory with eye exams and the thought of getting glasses was in kindergarden. At Jefferson elementary, my school in Medford, Oregon, we had our eyes tested every year. It was such an exciting day. All of us got to go into the gym and stand in line to wait our turn to look at the giant "E's." That's the way it was for us, at least. We would stand with one eye covered and look at a board of "E's" and have to point with our hand to the correct direction of the "E." As we got older we just read the letters we saw, but as a kindergartener we just said if the "E" was facing up, down, left, or right.

I remember the anticipation I felt as my turn was approaching. When it was finally my turn I covered my left eye as instructed and pointed with my hand to the direction the "E" was facing. My teacher looked pleased as I was able to read to the very tiniest of "E's" with my right eye. Then it was time to cover my right eye. I was feeling pretty confident at this point, but was caught off guard when I couldn't even read the biggest "E" on the sign! Within moments I had a note in my hand that stated I needed to go to the eye doctor.

My mom took me to the doctor that year, and every year following, to have my left eye examined. To my utter dismay, I always left the doctor's office without eye glasses! I wasn't able to read a single letter with my left eye, but was never given glasses! I remember wondering, "What does it take to get glasses?! I can't see a thing with my left eye, yet I never get a prescription." It was so discouraging. I longed to get a pair of cool glasses, but never could. Finally, one year I was sent to the doctor's, as I was every year, and decided to change things up. I was going to get glasses! As always, I couldn't see a thing with my left eye, but when they got to my right eye (which was incredibly sharp in its vision) I lied and said I couldn't read a thing.

I'll never forget sitting in the chair reading off the letters incorrectly to the doctor. I knew I was lying, and could see the letters perfectly with my right eye, but I wanted glasses! When we finished with the exam I was stunned to hear the doctor say, "She doesn't need glasses!" What?! How could that be?! I hadn't read a single line correctly! My left eye couldn't see a stinkin' thing, but I lied my way through my good eye … and still … no glasses!

Fast forward to the year 2010 (yes, it's been close to forty years since my previous story). I now was sitting in the doctor's office watching my four children have their eyes examined. I couldn't resist the urge to confess my story of lying about not being able to read the letters and still not getting glasses. The doctor informed me that it happens all the time … children lying in order to get those cool glasses. Then she told me technology has greatly improved since my generation (no offense intended).

I was eager to get myself into the chair and have her examine my eyes. No surprise, I could see perfectly with my right eye and not a lick out of my left … nope … not even the biggest letter! I assumed I would leave without glasses as I always had, but not this time! She told me I had amblyopia (a lazy eye) and there was a lens that could help me see in 3-D. I was puzzled at her comment and quickly informed her that I *could* see in 3-D. In detail I explained that I could clearly see that she was standing in front of the door, thus, I could see 3-D … or so I thought.

In the preceding minutes I was educated on 3-D vision, and how *both* eyes were required to create this visual ability. Living for close to forty years with only one functioning eye, I couldn't understand what it was she was trying to explain to me, but I wasn't overly concerned because … I WAS GETTING GLASSES! After years of leaving the doctor's office with one bad eye and no glasses, this visit was different. I was one of the cool people trying on "frames" as they call it. Whatever it's called … I liked it! After hours of trying on pretty much every pair of "frames" in the office, I had one chosen and awaited my glasses to wear home!

When the glasses were ready for pick up, I took all my kids with me to the office to pick them up. The doctor informed me that it was going to be a whole new world for me as I was going to see in 3-D for the first time. (I felt no reason to argue with her that I *could* see in 3-D … I knew that one object was in front of the other … to me … that was 3-D!) The moment I pulled into our driveway I put on my "I've-waited-thirty-five-years-to-get-these-super-cool-glasses!" It was at this moment that I wish you could have been me. It's difficult to explain, but I'll give it my best. I rounded the corner to our front door and passed by a bush near our house. I took one look at it and about had a heart attack! I jumped back and screamed for dear life at the sight in front of me! The bush was reaching out towards me! I had never seen anything so terrifying! My scream startled the kids and they ran to see what had happened. I wasn't sure how to explain it since everything happened so fast. Still horrified, I shouted out, "The bush scared me!" I felt ridiculous as the words left my mouth, but I couldn't deny it had … but why?

Once inside, I sat down to catch my breath and ponder how it was a shrub had frightened me. It was at that moment I had the next horror … the dogs! As I looked up to see my two dogs coming towards me I freaked out screaming and curled into a ball on my chair. I sat there with my eyes clenched shut and my arms wrapped tightly around my tucked up knees! What a frightening sight! My two sweet dogs, with tails wagging, coming for me to pet them. It was then that I realized what was happening … I was seeing in 3-D for the first time in my life! I had never seen anything coming *at* me (my dogs), or sticking *out* at me (the bush). As I cautiously opened my eyes, I began to look around at this new world. Everything was different. I had spent my entire life seeing in 2-D (flat like a photograph). Suddenly I was thrust into 3-D (like a movie people would watch at the theater with their 3-D glasses on). I remembered watching commercials for 3-D movies and they'd show the crowd wearing their glasses shrinking back in terror as something came at them. That is how I felt. Everything was coming at me for the first time. It was fascinating … and terrifying!

I looked at balls. They went from circles to spheres for the first time in my life. I looked at trees and the branches had dimension to them. Chandeliers seemed to be suspended in mid-air, like I had never seen. I would spend hours looking at my hands placing one in front of the other. There was "space" between them. I had never seen "space" before. Everything had dimension. I was in complete and total awe. How can you ever explain to someone "space" and "dimension" when all they can see is "flat?"

To be honest, I wouldn't trade that experience for a lifetime of seeing in 3-D. I was able to experience people's "normal" for the first time. It was an overwhelming, mind-blowing, indescribable experience. I would walk around my house saying, "the ball is round, the picture is sticking off of the wall, the flower has separate petals that stick out, the tree has branches that stick out, the swing set is in front of the fence, everything had dimension and space … everything!

No one could have convinced me, prior to my glasses, that I couldn't see 3-D, because I *thought* I knew what 3-D was. I thought it simply meant that you could tell if one object was in front of another, such as you could tell in a photograph. However, it is so much more than a photograph! It is indescribable to someone who cannot see it! It is amazing!

That is what I think Paul was trying to explain when he wrote the words found in 1 Corinthians 13:12 "For now we see only a reflection as in a mirror; then we shall see face to face. Now I know in part; then I shall know fully, even as I am fully known." How many questions do we have in regards to life? How many injustices have we seen that we shake our fist at God and ask, "WHY?!" We doubt His love. We doubt His mercy. We doubt His wisdom. We doubt Him. But let's consider the story I just mentioned about my silly glasses. I was so sure that I was seeing things accurately. I knew that I was seeing things as they were … but I wasn't. I was seeing through a flawed vision. Once the glasses came on, then I saw clearly. It made me realize that I do not see all things as they really are. God sees clearly, I see dimly. It allows me to trust that He has all things in His control. And one day, every question I have, every moment of confusion, all will be made clear when I see as Jesus sees. Until then, I'll trust that He sees all things clearly, and He will lead us safely to Him.

Printed in the United States
By Bookmasters